Focus on the 90%

Focus on the 90%

# Focus on the 90%
## One simple tool to change the way you view your life.

## by Darci Lang

# © Copyright 2012 by Darci Lang

## Distributed by

X-L Enterprises Inc.
P.O. Box 32077, Regina, SK S4N 6E0
Ph: (306) 569-1354 Fax: (306) 569-1356
E-mail: info@darcilang.com
**www.darcilang.com**

Cover design: brent pylot
Cover illustration: brent pylot
Photo of Darci Lang: Mark Greschner

Library and Archives Canada Cataloguing in Publication

Lang, Darci, 1969-
    Focus on the 90%: one simple tool to change the way you view your life / Darci Lang.

ISBN 978-0-9783157-2-6

    1. Attitude change. 2. Optimism. 3. Self-actualization (Psychology)
I. Title.

BF637.S4L3535 2007          158.1          C2007-901540-9

Focus on the 90%

Focus on the 90%

# Acknowledgements

Thank you:

To my husband Darren – I am your greatest fan. Together forever, and this day.

To the most amazing children in the world, Jayda and John – I love you and I am so blessed God picked me to be your mom.

To my many "extended families" and friends who continue to love and support me.

To my admin assistant Sandra who gets me out the door and back. Nineteen years later, I am so grateful to be on this journey with you.

To all the wonderful audience members I have met, and continue to meet and to those whose stories fill this book – you touch my life in ways you will never know.

And above all, thank you God – thank you for every day I wake healthy with fingers able to type and a heart eager to share my message with those who are ready to hear it. Thanks for the words you give me to say and for inspiring me to do what I do. Thank you for helping me to stay focused on the 90%s in my own world.

Focus on the 90%

# **Contents**

Focus on the 90%

*"When you change the way you look at things, the things you look at change."*
Wayne Dyer

# Introduction:
# The positive 90% idea

My hope is that this book will offer you one single idea that will help you to live a happier life. Not nineteen ways or six ideas. ***Just one – Focus on the 90% that is positive in your life, rather than the 10% that is not.*** This one tool is enough to change your life. Focusing on the positive 90% has changed mine.

I believe we hold an imaginary magnifying glass out in front of us and we can choose to do two things with that magnifying glass. We can **choose** to focus it on the positive 90%s in our lives that work, or we can choose to focus it on the negative 10%s that don't work. What we focus on determines how we live our lives.

Everyone has 10%s in his or her life. I am a happy person but I am not delusional, I understand life is not perfect. But I find too often, people get pre-occupied with what they don't like about themselves, or their spouse or their jobs. Dwelling on these 10%s can be exhausting and only serves to distract you from the 90% that you love about yourself and others around you.

Why isn't 90% good enough? When you were in school, if you got 90% on an exam I'll bet you were pretty happy (or at least 90% of you were). We are not perfect, our spouse isn't perfect, nor are our children, friends, co-workers or jobs. We discover true peace of mind and a lot happier life when we learn to accept this and start focusing on the 90% that works.

In this book, I will challenge you to ask yourself whether you hold your magnifying glass on the positive 90% or the negative 10% when it comes to all areas of your life. I cover five areas in this book. I ask whether you focus on the 90% or the 10% when it comes to **yourself, your family, the people around you, your job and your clients**.

**What do you focus on when it comes to yourself?** No one is perfect. Are you trying too hard to be? Do you tend to focus on your 10% negatives and not your own 90% positives? Let's make life easier for ourselves. With stress and depression at an all time high, how can we learn to focus more on what is good about ourselves? How can we learn to reframe our belief systems and what we learned at our dinner tables?

**What do you focus on with your family?** Many people tend to give 90% at work and 10% at home. In this book, we will talk about having something left for the people we love. Whatever family represents to you, we have a choice as to how we treat our family at the end of the day.

**What about the people around you?** Most agree that a negative person can bring down a group. So what do we do with those "10%ers" around us? Since we can only control ourselves, not others, how can we learn to exist successfully among people who are unhappy? How can we learn to see others through our 90% magnifying glass?

**What do you focus on within your job?** Have you ever met anyone who complains about their job? In this chapter we will talk about what happens when we take a negative attitude to our workplaces. What happens to us and the people who have to work with us? We will talk about the "ripple effect" of a negative attitude at work. How can we learn to find the positive 90%s in our job?

**What about your clients/customers?** We all have accountability to our businesses or organizations to give our clients the best possible service. This includes those clients who just seem to be unhappy no matter what service level we provide to them. We put unrealistic expectations on ourselves and our staff to think "the customer is always right." 10% of the time the customer is "not right", they are just cranky no matter what we might do for them.

**We read motivational books and we see speakers share their messages on staying positive. We hear great information that we know we should apply to our lives but often it just seems too overwhelming. We are totally motivated at least until the car ride home. We get too many ideas and just not enough time.**

**That's why I wanted to give you one idea in this book. Focusing on the positive 90% not on the negative 10%. It is one simple idea that has made a world of difference in my life.**

**One thing I have discovered is that life is really short. As I write the fourth edition of this book I am 43 years old. It feels like only yesterday I was 18 years old (with the same hairdo)! I want to spend the rest of my life happy and living each day ... ok, 90% of my days ... to the fullest. I don't want to be at the end my life saying I wish I would have ... I should have.**

**We really do have a choice about the attitude we have towards ourselves, our families, others and our jobs. Let your choice be a positive 90% one.**

*"Individuals who are positive in their thoughts always tend to look upon the brighter side of life. With their faces turned toward the sunshine, they attempt to see the good, even in the bad. Such individuals habitually think thoughts of a positive nature and they are a blessing to this world. They are in a positive vibration, and therefore attract other positive personalities to them."*
Bob Proctor, Author and Speaker

# Dottie

I have learned many lessons about the importance of focusing on the positive 90%s in life. I have also learned many, I wish I would have/should have lessons as well. Choosing to see the positive 90% in yourself is not an easy task. Choosing to see the positives in others can be difficult too.

This story is important to me because it not only shows the focusing on the 90% idea in action, but the event itself really helped me to understand this idea and just how powerful it can be.

Let me tell you about my mother-in-law, Dorothy. My husband Darren's Dad passed away when he was just eight years old leaving "Dottie" to raise her three boys. Darren is the baby boy of a Roman Catholic mother.

Let's just say that when I first met my mother-in-law, we did not see eye-to-eye. She had a tendency to "over mother" me and I locked my magnifying glass on the 10% of Dottie that rubbed me the wrong way and that is all I could see. I was not her first choice as a mate for her baby either. I was broke and had never been to church a day in my life. Not exactly what she was hoping for. Though she was always very nice to me, it just did not start out well. Darren and I bought a house close to her, but I didn't respect her the way I should have.

Months later, my beloved grandmother, Nan, passed away. I remember sitting at her funeral thinking, I wish I would have … I should have. My grandmother was one of the most important people in my childhood and I did not tell her enough how much I loved her and how much I appreciated all she did for me. I remember that quiet three hour drive home from the funeral with Darren. I remember sitting in that passenger seat thinking, I never want to do that again. I never want to sit at the funeral of another person, wishing I would have and I should have. I decided to make a mental list of who else's funeral I would be likely to sit at and say that. The first person to pop into my mind was Dottie.

I thought about it for most of that ride and then I said to Darren, "You know what. When we get into the city, drop me off at your mom's. I want to talk to her." He looked at me and said in a worried voice, "Why?" I told him not to worry, I just wanted to clear the air.

When Dottie opened the door and asked how the funeral was, I told her the story. I told her how I thought of her on the way home and did not ever want to say, I wish I would have and I should have with her. I asked her to forgive me and ... that loving Christian woman did.

We started with a clean slate and I made a choice to start seeing her positive 90%s. Sure, she still over-mothered me and popped into our house whenever she felt like it, but there were so many positives about her.

She shared great stories about the joys and hardships of being the oldest of 13 siblings on a dairy farm. She talked about her late husband John and how much she loved and missed him. She talked about when he got sick and how hard it was to care for a dying husband. I started to really admire this woman. She had a grade eight education when John died, and while raising her three boys and working full time, she earned a university degree. She loved to shop and travel and had over 200 pairs of shoes.

I am a very conservative dresser while she loved anything red and anything with sequins on it. We had opposite tastes in dress. She bought me red clothing that I never dared wear. My closet contains more red clothing than I can count! She didn't like my hair down. She thought I should wear it up. "It is much prettier that way", she often told me.

Every time we go on a road trip for a speaking engagement she calls and leaves a long message on our phone telling us the same thing every time. "Be careful! If you see something up ahead on the highway slow down until you know what it is, many lives were saved on the farm by slowing down." I could recite the message word for word I had heard it so many times. It drove me crazy!

I love this woman. I know we still get on each other's nerves but we accept and love each other. Our bond is the wonderful man she raised, our Darren. I often think about how without her, I wouldn't have him. Dottie was not raised to be a hugger. I was. So I always left her with a hug and told her I loved her. She always hugged back and said the same.

In 2001, Dottie, passed away suddenly from an aneurysm. We never got to say good-bye.

The first thing that came to my mind was Thank God. Thank God I made a choice and moved my magnifying glass. Thank God I told her I loved her the last time I saw her. No regrets. I miss her so much. The things I miss the most are her pop in visits, my red clothing and I really miss that message on my answering machine as I pack up to leave for a road trip.

I delivered a portion of the family eulogy at her funeral. It was by far the toughest speaking "gig" of my life. Four hundred and fifty people packed the church on that sunny July day. Her favourite pink flowers lined the big altar - the same altar where I was baptized and married. Dottie's beloved Sweet Adelines' sang, "I am the Bread of Life" as her casket was wheeled up to the altar. It was one of the most emotional days of my life. I wondered how I would keep it together and deliver the eulogy.

It was my turn to speak. I walked to the altar. To honor Dottie I wore the most amazing red suit. I wore a sequin shirt underneath. I wore my hair up. I looked like a hooker!

I stood in front of that group of 450 people and I said:

*"Let's each live our life like Dottie did. Let's live our life so that 450 people attend our funeral and miss us as much as we will miss her.*

*"Let's go and live our lives so that we never say … I wish I would have … I should have … Let's tell the people we love that we do love them every day so that you will never wish you had.*

*"I will never regret the time I had with this amazing woman. I will never forget how she shaped the woman I am today. She is a true example to all of us that life is short and is so precious.*

*"Leave this church today with an attitude that you will never regret. You will say sorry, you will forgive and you will love. Let's live each day like it may be our last."*

I will always be grateful I moved my magnifying glass off the 10% of Dottie that bothered me and onto the 90% that was wonderful, loving and supportive. This simple shift in perspective gave me one of the most precious relationships I have ever had ... and I could have missed it. It lets me look back on our time together with no regrets, just fond memories.

So how can focusing on the 90% positive work for you? Let's take a closer look at the 90% idea and discuss how it can help you live a happier and more connected life with fewer regrets.

*"You only live once but if you live right, once is enough. "*
Adam Marshall

# Yourself

Not everyone is going to like you. At least 10% won't. But the happier you are with yourself the less likely their opinion will have an affect on you. People, who are unhappy in their job and with others, tend to be unhappy with themselves too.

How we feel about ourselves relates to how we interact with others. It starts with us. You know the saying "you can't love anyone until you love yourself?" I only partly agree with this, we can love others if we don't love ourselves, however, we can love them more fully if we love ourselves first.

As children we are taught that focusing on the positive 90%s of ourselves is bragging. Saying a simple thank you to someone when they say they like what you are wearing is hard for many people. Some people tell me that they grew up in families that taught them to down play their positives. Perhaps we call that a form of humility.

I used to do a workshop in my presentations where I would ask people to share a 90% positive about themselves in front of the group. I stopped doing that because so many people would tell me they were not comfortable doing that ... or worse, they had nothing to say.

I am not perfect. I don't want to be. The people that I know in my life who are trying to be perfect are missing out on life along the way. I am only 90%, in all respects.

I have learned to accept my 10%s and move on. We have many 90%s. Honor yourself and your positive attributes.

*"Your outlook on life is a direct reflection of how much you like yourself."*
lululemon athletica

My sister-in-law told me what a woman said at their annual block party BBQ. One of her neighbors asked:

"Are you related to Darci Lang, the speaker?" When my sister-in-law responded, "Yes", her neighbor said, "She must be perfect." My sister-in-law said to me, "Don't worry. I told her for fifteen minutes that you aren't!"

My initial thought was, I'm glad she said that because no one is perfect and I don't want anyone walking around thinking that.

It wasn't until later that I thought ... hey, wait a minute, that wasn't really a compliment was it? Ha ha! (And I still love my sister-in-law!)

*I rarely watch television but I love a comedy movie. I believe in surrounding myself with positive books, movies, etc. You are what you surround yourself with.*

*One of my favorite movies is the 1987 classic, "Planes, Trains and Automobiles" starring Steve Martin and the late John Candy. If you haven't seen this movie – you must! If you have, you will remember the hotel room scene. (I am not talking about the pillows, but that is very funny!) The scene where Steve Martin lashes out at John Candy telling him how worthless he is? I love the part where John Candy with full sincerity looks at Steve Martin and says "My friends like me, my wife likes me, I am the real article, what you see is what you get."*

# The Cracked Pot (A tale from India)

A water bearer in India had two large pots, each hung on one end of a pole, which he carried across his neck. One of the pots had a crack in it, and while the other pot was perfect and always delivered a full portion of water at the end of the long walk from the stream to the master's house, the cracked pot arrived only half full.

For a full two years this went on daily, with the bearer delivering only one and a half pots full of water to his master's house. Of course, the perfect pot was proud of its accomplishments, perfect to the end for which it was made. But the poor cracked pot was ashamed of its own imperfection, and miserable that it was able to accomplish only half of what it had been made to do.

After two years of what it perceived to be a bitter failure, it spoke to the water bearer one day by the stream. "I am ashamed of myself, and I want to apologize to you." "Why?" asked the bearer. "What are you ashamed of?" "I have been able, for these past two years, to deliver only half my load because this crack in my side causes water to leak out all the way back to your master's house. Because of my flaws, you have to do all of this work, and you don't get full value from your efforts," the pot said.

The water bearer said to the pot, "Did you ever notice the beautiful flowers along the path? Did you notice that there were flowers only on your side of the path, but not on the other pot's side? That's because I have always known about your flaw, and I took advantage of it. I planted flower seeds on your side of the path, and every day while we walk back from the stream, you've watered them. For two years I have been able to pick these beautiful flowers to decorate the house."

Each of us has our unique flaws. We are all cracked pots. It is our flaws that make us unique and special.

*What makes you special? Create a 90% list for yourself. List all of your positive attributes.*

*Give it to your friends and loved ones and ask them to tell you why you are special. When you are having a 10% day ... read your 90% list and the comments you have gathered.*

*"No matter what age you are, or what your circumstances might be, you are special, and you still have something unique to offer. Your life, because of who you are, has meaning."*
Barbara de Angelis

# Let's start at the beginning

Where does how we feel about ourselves start? Most would say our childhood and I would have to agree. The dinner table we grew up at strongly influences our belief system and who we are today. Many people tell me that their childhood is what has shaped them and how they feel about themselves. Very few people I have met say they had the "perfect childhood." How we see our childhood is how we perceive it. If we view it through our 10% magnifying glass we only see the unhappiness ... if we learn ... (key word "learn") ... to move our magnifying glass to the "90%s" we start to see the positives.

I was born in 1969 in a small Saskatchewan town called "Biggar." Biggar is a very optimistic town. 2600 people live in Biggar and the sign outside of town reads, "New York is Big, but this is Biggar." My young parents Beverley and John did not stay together and through the years have been married three times each. Ten of us children have come together in those five marriages.

For many years, I viewed my childhood through my 10% magnifying glass. I spent many years "blaming" my childhood for my life.

At 24 years of age I had a "Quarter-Life Crisis." (It's great now because I don't have to have a Mid-Life Crisis. I'm done!) While the tuxedo company I was working at was going under, I felt I was going under too. I was broke, unhealthy (basically destroying myself) and very unhappy. I was feeling very sorry for myself.

I remember during that time I called my dad. I told him I was sitting in my rented dirt basement house, like the one he and I had lived in. I told him that it was interesting irony that life puts you right back where you started. I also told him that I was blaming him for the mess I was in. I told him, if it wasn't for the childhood I'd had, I would be better able to deal with my life.

My "tough love" dad said to me over the phone, "You know what Darc? You can only blame your parents until you are 18 years old. You made that mess you are living in … now go clean it up."

I was not very happy with my dad at the time for that reaction. But I am now. I think if it were not for that call, I would still be living in that dirt basement house blaming everyone else for my life. I had no one left to blame but me. I decided he was right; I needed to clean up my life. I looked at the only woman I could change, the one staring back at me in the mirror.

I went and got some counseling. I had met so many people in my life who were unhappy because of their past. Some people carry those issues around like luggage for the rest of their lives. I've met people in their 50s who were still blaming their parents for their lives.

I started to read motivational books and I read a book called "Attitude is Your Most Priceless Possession" by Elwood Chapman. I picked it up and opened a page. As Oprah would say it was my "Light Bulb Moment." It said, "We hold a magnifying glass out in front of us and we can choose what we focus it on."

That book started to change my perspective on how I viewed my job and the people around me. Most importantly it started to change how I viewed my past and myself personally. I carried this imaginary magnifying glass around and challenged myself to see the 90%s.

Ten percent of my childhood was not positive ... but 90% was. I had spent so many years playing back the movie of my childhood with my magnifying glass stuck on the 10%s that I couldn't see the positives. And there were so many.

For example: when you are raised by that many parents, do you know how many grandparents that added up to? Christmas was amazing; I just went from house to house and "raked it in." I had many different houses to visit! You can imagine how blessed our children are with all of the grandparents they have. We start celebrating Christmas mid-November to make sure we fit in all of our families!

My friend Jean said, "You made a choice to put the FUN back into dysfunctional."

### *So many people were positive in my life:*

My grandparents – Nan and Pop – taught me unconditional love. I miss them. My summer holidays at their house, playing with my cousins, are the happiest memories of my childhood.

My dad taught me how to hug and tell people that you love them. His motto was to never leave anyone you love without telling them you love them first. He taught me to be a communicator. He taught me perseverance, a strong work ethic and how to be an entrepreneur. He also taught me … girls can do anything they want to do.

My mom, Beverley, taught me forgiveness. Life is too short to carry around burdens that do not bless your life, or the lives of others. My mom, who has since passed away, was a survivor in every sense of the word and she taught me strength. She is an example to me of living life full.

My stepmom, Sandy, raised me like her own daughter and taught me so many things. Most of all she taught me to see the good in others and that people need to live their life the way that is best for them. She raised me through my 10% teenage years and still loves me!

Each stepparent, aunt and uncle that touched my life loved me and taught me a bit of them.

I am the oldest child from the original "union" of parents. Each one of my step and half brothers and sisters taught me what it is like to love a child. They have shaped the mother I am today.

Sure, the 10%s are still there ... they always will be. The past cannot be changed. I have made a choice to forgive people and move on. I made a choice to focus on the 90%s.

I had an audience member hand me a small card. It read: **"Forgiveness is giving up the hope that the past can ever be different."** But the future can be different when you change your focus to the 90%.

*What are the positives of your childhood? What are your happiest memories? It becomes such a habit to see our childhoods through our 10% magnifying glass. Even if your childhood was a tragic one, there must be one or two 90%s ...*

"If you don't like something, change it, if you can't change it, change the way you see it."
Maya Angelou

# The Catholic Experience

I have made a lot of mistakes in my life. Things I wished I wouldn't have...things I should have. Many parts of my early adult life I wish I could just erase, but they too have shaped who I am today. I could probably write another book just on those mistakes! As I look back I have seen the lessons along the way. Everything that I did and everything that happened to me I now know was part of the journey. I learned at my dinner table growing up that it was ok to make a mistake. I learned that just because you make a mistake does not mean you are one.

I had always dated the same guy, different hairdo. Then I met my husband Darren. I became many things when I met Darren: first, I became the luckiest woman in the world. I also became two other things – a Catholic and the wife of a raving Saskatchewan Roughrider Football Fan. Both of which require a lot of praying and forgiveness! Ha ha!

Prior to meeting Darren, I had never been to church a day in my life. Especially a Catholic Church! I always joked that you never wanted to go to a Catholic wedding because you would be there all day! Darren and I wanted to start our relationship on a positive note so we came together with our list of what we were looking for in a husband and wife and at the top of Darren's list was, "She needs to be a Roman Catholic." He was everything on my list so I decided I would give this religion thing a try!

I remember the first time I attended church with Darren. I expected to see a 200-year-old priest bent over the altar reading Latin bible verses for three or four hours. Instead, I was greeted by a handsome priest with a huge smile who looked at me, looked at Darren and said, "Where did you pick her up?" Father Joe Balzer, "Balzer" as Darren called him, was one of the nicest men I've ever met. Church was a wonderful eye-opener. I saw families with five and six children, all from the same mother and father ... what a concept!

For eight months, Darren and I attended RCIA classes (Rite of Christian Initiation for Adults). These classes would prepare me for my baptism that Easter. The late Father Joe Balzer, Deacon Joe Lang and their team taught me many things in that time. While I took away many great life lessons, the greatest thing I learned was the ability to **forgive others as you have been forgiven.** Most importantly, forgive yourself too. It was truly a life changing experience for me and my "cradle Catholic" Darren. It opened up spiritual gifts I never knew I had.

I remember standing at that altar ready to be baptized on Easter weekend with my family and friends in the pews. Father Balzer leaned over and whispered in my ear, "Hey Darc, this is your chance to wash away all of your sins." I whispered back with a smile, "Do you think we have that kind of time?"

*The Serenity Prayer*

*God grant me the serenity to accept the things I cannot change*
*The courage to change the things I can*
*And the wisdom to know the difference.*

## Forgiveness

I don't read the paper but Darren does, so often I grab the paper out of the mailbox and scan the front page to see what is going on in the world. The front page story caught my attention. A brave woman was speaking at a local church about her terrifying childhood of abuse and how she turned her life around.

Her words stayed with me, "I forgive my parents for what they did to me because if someone hadn't done it to them, they wouldn't have done it to me."

It takes some people a lifetime to forgive. What a courageous choice she has made to see the 90%s in a 10% past.

## You aren't happy?

I love reading motivational books. I love filling myself with positive. It is definitely one of the ways I invest in my own happiness. I read in a Christian book a story similar to this.

If our children came to us and said they were unhappy, we would be disappointed. Well I know I would be! If our special Jayda and John came to me and said they were not happy with their life I would say "**WHAT?** You have a healthy Mom and Dad who pick you up from school everyday and lie in your bed at night and tell you how much they love you. You have a van with a DVD in the roof - unlike the VW van I grew up with! You have more toys than we can store, endless technical gadgets and a warm safe house." I would be very sad if they were not grateful for their 90% life.

I think when we are not happy for our lives God feels the same way. He says, "**WHAT?** I give you the greatest country in the world to live in, your health, a job, a family to love and the eyes to read this book and you still aren't happy?"

*"Circumstances and situations do color life, but you have been given the mind to choose what the color shall be."*
John Homer Miller

## How much is enough?

We have talked about focusing on the positive 90% of your past. Now let's talk about the present. I think one of the most stressful things we do to ourselves is the endless pursuit of the 10% that we do not have. We are consumed with what we do not have rather than what we do have. If you have ever been to a big box store on a Saturday, you know what I mean. I feel blessed to come from very little material wealth. It taught me to appreciate all that I have.

My house is not perfect. I live in middle class suburbia in a house as old as I am. I love our house. When were first married, Darren and I have painted every wall and I sewed every curtain. Years ago we saved and scrimped to buy this house, our dream home back then. We have carried two beautiful newborns through the door and are raising our children in our amazing tree-lined back yard. We have the greatest neighbors who are dear friends ... something you don't always get! We still have Jayda and John's crafts framed all over the house. Our fridge door is overflowing with pictures of family members and friends.

We have family pictures displayed all over our house, and the challenge is to arrange them so the visiting family is up front!! Everyone who visits says, "This is a house you can really live in!" (I choose to take that as a compliment!)

We have friends and family who say, "Why don't you move into someplace bigger/newer/nicer?" I always answer "Why?" To me, the endless pursuit of more wastes the time I could be living. Besides, I can't keep clean the size of house that I already have!

I honestly think that being happy with what you have is one of the secrets to happiness. I intentionally live well below my means. I would rather work less, eat organic food, go to Hawaii and buy shoes!! Why do I need a bigger house? Sure I like nice things but I am not willing to pay the price, literally or figuratively.

*My Darren has a t-shirt from Hawaii and on the front it says "No Rain, No Rainbows." The back of the t-shirt has motivational sayings listed under the heading "Kimo's Hawaiian Rules." One line reads: "There are two ways to be rich, make more, or desire less."*

## Grateful

Traveling home on a delayed flight I caught myself focusing on the 10%s. I was at the end of a long traveling schedule and feeling a little weary. We arrived home in the middle of the night to freezing cold weather, late luggage and a half an hour wait for a taxi. Though I was chanting 90% … 90% in my head, I was feeling sorry for myself as I stood one of the last people in the airport waiting for a ride.

I could see the taxi driver smiling as he pulled up to the airport. He jumped out and carefully loaded my suitcases in his car. His energy was infectious. We exchanged the usual pleasantries. I wasn't really in the mood for talking (very unlike me – just ask my husband!) but I wanted to know more about this happy man on this dark cold night.

He told me how he had just moved to Canada with his wife and their four children. He went on and on about how lucky he was to have found his job and how blessed we are to live here. He told me funny stories of his children seeing snow for the first time. They had rented an apartment and he raved about how lucky we are to have homes of our own. He told me his parents would join them next year. When I asked if he would need to rent a house instead of the apartment for extra room, he seemed shocked at the idea. He said with sincerity "oh no, we have plenty of room for everyone."

As we pulled up to my middle class house, he sat back and said, "Wow, you live in a palace – you are a lucky woman." I gave him an extra big tip and crept into my sleeping house.

I sat quietly on the front bench to pet our cat, Isabella, and took a minute to Focus on my 90%s. I have a job that I love. I get to travel; some people have never been on an airplane. I live in a safe beautiful city, however cold, to raise our children in. We own our home and though older, it is our house, even a palace to some. I have my health, something I never take for granted. I have a healthy sleeping family to come home to. I went into their rooms and kissed their sleeping faces. I went to sleep very grateful.

*"Can you see the holiness in those things you take for granted – a paved road or a washing machine? If you concentrate on finding what is good in every situation, you will discover that your life will suddenly be filled with gratitude, a feeling that nurtures the soul."*
Rabbi Harold Kushner

## It could always be worse.

On another trip, I was leaving the hotel to catch a cab to my presentation. I was shocked awake by a -47 degree Celsius wind chill temperature. If you are from the Prairies, you have lived that!

There were four of us huddled outside the hotel doors, all waiting for our warm cabs. The two people to my right were complaining non-stop about the cold, the wind, and the weather. The gentleman to my left waited quietly.

A cab pulled up and we all anxiously waited to see who's name the driver would call. It was Glen, the quiet man to my left. He loaded his bag into the back and before he jumped into his taxi, he looked at the complaining two and yelled out, "Hey complain all you want; there is no malaria!"

We all burst out laughing. Good point on this cold day. There are still 90%s.

It is easy to slip sometimes and focus on the 10%s, what we don't have, what we wish we had and start to feel sorry for ourselves. It is wonderful how God always puts someone in my path during those times to remind me of what is really important and how grateful I should be.

*What are you grateful for? Stop and take a deep breath right now and reflect on your 90%s.*

*"Feeling gratitude and not expressing it is like wrapping a present and not giving it."*
William Arthur Ward

## What happens if we don't learn to focus on the 90%s?

Bob, Candace and their two small boys lived in our old neighborhood years ago. Candace was a happy, beautiful woman and a wonderful mother who loved being a stay-at-home mom. Bob was more reserved but friendly enough. One thing that really stood out about Bob was that he was a perfectionist. Many times I drove by, watching his boys play as he worked, and I hoped he took the time to play with them too.

Now don't get me wrong, I am a "doer"! I never sit still but I have learned how to stop and just "be."

I noticed a "For Sale" sign on Bob and Candace's lawn. I found out they had bought a brand new house in a more affluent neighborhood. I slipped a card in the mailbox wishing them well and telling them we would miss them. We lost touch.

A couple of years later I was in the grocery store shopping without my children. When our children were toddlers, I called this "an outing." As I turned the corner to head down an aisle I spotted someone familiar, it was Candace. I stopped in my tracks as I got closer to her. Candace was still as beautiful as ever, but I could tell something was wrong.

We were the only two in the aisle and we met half way. She looked up and we made eye contact. I didn't have to ask how she was ... I could see it in her eyes. I walked closer and asked her, "Candace is everything all right?" She started crying, standing in the middle of the grocery store aisle crying her eyes out. Now I was crying too, and I don't even know why we are crying. We are now hugging too, in the middle of the aisle.

Out of the corner of my eye, I can see some men coming up the aisle. They see us crying and hugging and make one big 90 degree turn and head the other way! Whatever our problem was, they were not coming near us! I imagine they were a few things short of a full load of groceries when they went home that day!

As we regained our composure she asked me if I had time to talk. She said, "Darci. This is so weird. I was thinking about you this week. I wanted to call you and share a story with you." She dug out Kleenex and juice boxes from her shopping cart. We sat right on the bottom shelf in the middle of that grocery aisle and talked.

Candace started by saying: *I have a story for your presentation about what happens if you keep focusing on the 10%s instead of the 90%s. You must have noticed Bob's personality, how obsessive he is. The way he is with the yard is the way he is with everything else in his life. Nothing is ever good enough for Bob. That is why we bought the new house, new cars and new furniture. Stuff we couldn't really afford. I was really happy in our old house but he wanted to "keep up"*

31

*with the Jones'. I really think it goes back to his dad. He was never good enough in the eyes of his parents and he has spent years trying to measure up. The belief system he learned at the dinner table was that he had to be perfect.*

*Bob manages 15 people in his job and 14 of his employees love him. One doesn't. All he talks about is how he can make that one person happy. His customers love him but he obsesses over the 10% that he doesn't serve perfectly. Then Darci, when Bob comes home at the end of the day, we are never good enough. The house is never cleaned to his perfect standards. Now the boys are in school he expects them to excel in everything. We have so many positive 90%s in our lives but he cannot see them! He is so wrapped up in his obsessive behavior that he is missing all the great things.*

*Well Darci, last year Bob did it to himself. I knew it was just a matter of time before it all got to him and sure enough, it happened. He started to get worse and worse. He started sleeping a lot and snapping at us all the time. He started to call in sick to work and watch television all day. Not like Bob at all. Finally his boss told him he needed to take a break for a while. When he was off, he just started slipping away. I begged him to get help but he was too proud. He finally went to see a counselor who diagnosed him with depression and suggested he try some medication. Bob was too proud to take a pill. No man in his family would ever do that.*

*It's a big mess. I have lost my husband and the boys have lost their dad. It has been so hard on all of us. I have told Bob if he doesn't do something to make himself feel better, I am going to leave.*

*The reason I wanted to call you Darci is because Bob's story is a living example of what happens when you only focus on 10%s. When your magnifying glass can only see what is not right or good in your life, you miss out on all the positive 90%s along the way. Something the counselor told Bob was if he had only gotten the help he needed earlier ... when he felt himself slipping ... he would not be in the state he is now.*

*He said something that really made me think of you, Darci. He told Bob, 'If you feel overwhelmed, you are'.*

Our 10%s grow to be our 90%s if we do not take care of them. My Darren will share his story later in this book about how not dealing with his 10%s lead to more too.

***Ask yourself if you are overwhelmed. What can you do about it? Do you need counselling? A doctor visit? Do you need help?***

## Triple Espresso

I don't drink coffee very often and when I do, I'm like Jerry Seinfeld; I get my coffee on the outside.

One day, I arrived at my local coffee shop and walked passed the only other vehicle in the parking lot, a big truck with a construction company logo on the side. I got in line inside behind a big burly tough looking guy whose appearance matched his truck. He was dressed in construction boots and coveralls, his neck and hands tanned from working outside. I could just feel the tension coming off of him.

In a tired voice he ordered a coffee with three espresso shots in it. I thought I had heard him wrong. Obviously the woman behind the counter did too as she asked him to repeat it. He explained to her that he wanted her to put the espresso into the coffee to make it stronger. She joked with him saying, "Stronger is not the word." He just looked blankly at her as if to say, "Just get me my coffee."

He paid for his coffee, walked to the area where the cream was, put cream in his coffee. He stood at the counter and drank the entire cup and walked out.

All I could think was … wow! What is going on in this guy's life that he needs this kind of caffeine injection? From inside the coffee shop I could see him approach his truck. He could not see me but I watched him get in, sit down and put his head down on his steering wheel. I watched his shoulders shake and realized that he was crying. After a few moments he lifted his head and looked around to be sure no one had seen him. He wiped his eyes with the back of his hand and drove away.

I watched that tough guy and I thought of Bob. This guy has to go back to his construction site and pretend like everything is ok. He was clearly overwhelmed. I prayed that he would seek the help he needed to get through whatever he was dealing with. I also prayed that someone at work might notice his sadness and offer a listening ear. We often ignore the employees that seem to have pain; I hope his boss noticed his.

*Getting help takes courage. Don't be too proud or too tough to ask for what you need. I meet a lot of men who learned at their dinner tables growing up that men do not ask for help. Maybe what you learned at the dinner table was wrong. Is it time to ask for help?*

*"The healthy and strong individual is the one who asks for help when he needs it. Whether he's got an abscess on his knee or one in his soul."*
Rona Barrett

# Three times complain rule

Here is my deal about stress. Whether it is stress from the past, future or the present, consider the three times complain rule.

I have a huge family as a result of my childhood. I am blessed with a circle of really amazing friends. My deal with them is this: I have a "three times complain" rule. The rule is that I will lovingly listen to their concerns, challenges, stresses – their 10%s – three times. Everyone needs to vent. (Especially us women.) My dad taught me at a very young age it is not healthy to keep your stresses bottled up.

Three times friends or family can come to my table and I will honor them and whatever their stress is. I will hug them, cry with them and feed them. I will not offer advice or give them a seminar (which is hard for me)! I will just listen and be there for them.

BUT ... if they come a fourth time, I am going to ask them this: What are you going to do about it now?

I will ask them to lay their problem/stress out on the table and make an action plan to deal with it. "Lay that sucker out" is the way I say it. I will challenge them to ask themselves: Do they need help dealing with this problem? Do they need to have a talk with someone? Do they need marriage counseling? A parenting class? A new job? Is it something from the past they cannot solve? It isn't healthy for us to carry around the same stress for days, weeks or even years, and not take any action to solve it!

I have seen people try to avoid these problems by drugging, drinking, eating, shopping, gambling and a variety of other avoidances. The problems do not go away, they grow into bigger problems. I know people who have access to work Employee Assistance Programs at work and they never use them. There isn't a thing you have been through – or are going through - that you can't search for on the computer and get help with. The library is full of free books that can help you. Eckhart Tolle in his book "Power of Now" says, "You can trace all addictions back to a lack of self love."

I speak from the experience of carrying around many of my own stresses for years until I finally had to say … Enough! So one by one I laid those "suckers" out and I dealt with them. You know, some of what I laid out and took a good look at, I couldn't solve anyway. So I learned how to GET OVER IT and got on with living. I love the saying "It is what it is." Some problems "are what they are" and we need to change how we react to them and get on with our lives!

I often say to myself, "If this is my current reality and I can't change it, what can I do to make it better?"

Besides, I can't get away with complaining to my family and friends more than three times either!

Venting turns into plain old complaining when we say the same thing over and over and over again. And don't we all know someone who has complained a lot and had never choose to do something about it?

I think complaining more than three times is what one of my audience members called "recreational whining"

Waiting in an airport one day, I struck up a conversation with the woman beside me. For some reason, we got on the topic of being children of divorced parents. She said to me, "I was 15 when my parents divorced and I never got over it." I smiled and said, "You're 45 years old now, it's time."

***What suckers do you need to lay out? Lay them out one by one and do not try to tackle too many at once. You can only deal with one at a time. Go easy on yourself and ask for help if you need it.***

*"There are times in life when, instead of complaining, you do something about your complaints."*
Rita Dove

*I love to ask people what they are working in their personal development journey. I am always intrigued when people say they are not working on anything. I always wonder what it would be like to wake up and be "done."*

*I wonder when people tell me they are working on "nothing" if they are truly done or are they avoiding what they need to do. If I asked their coworkers and family members if they felt that this person needed to work on any personal issues, would they agree this person was perfect?*

*There are many who share with me what they are working on. My audience members will tell me they want more balance, they want to feel healthier, they want to be more peaceful etc. So my challenge to them is to START. Start today. Take baby steps towards what you want to do. Turn off the TV and the computer and create more balance, eat healthier, go to bed when you are tired. Starting is the hardest part.*

*I am a wounded healer, which connects me to many of my audience members. I think it is great to have had wounds to learn from but I think we are far greater healers if we are healing our own wounds too.*

*I truly believe that what we do not "work on", we will pass onto our children. We pass our unhappiness, insecurities and unfinished childhood issues onto them. Then they will need to work on these issues in their own adult lives. I hope to save my children some of the work I have had to do!*

*When people tell me their children are not happy I often ask, "Are you?" Are we showing our children what happiness looks like or are we telling them to be something we are not? We can give them the gift of letting them see what it looks like to care for ourselves. Can there be a better way for them to learn?*

## Just one thing

I over heard two women talking in line at the grocery store and one woman asked the other if she had made any News Years Resolutions? She replied "Oh why bother, I have so many things I want to improve and I never stick to them anyway."

Could I relate to that! I found in the past that I did not stick to my resolutions either. Just like the woman in line at the grocery store, I felt there were just too many things, too many "10%s" I wanted to improve. At the start of a year I would buy a lovely flowered journal and "lay out" what I wanted to resolve to do better in the upcoming year. I wanted to be healthier, build a stronger marriage with Darren, more quality time with Jayda and John, more time with family and friends, internal healing work, etc., etc. I would look back at the journal throughout the year and there seemed to be too many things.

So here is what I did a few years ago. I decided I would only work on one thing a year. I would spend the entire year working on just that one thing.

People ask me, "Where do I start?" Sit by yourself for a few minutes and think about your biggest stress – your burning issue – your greatest "10%." What is it? Your self-esteem? Health? Money? A relationship that needs mending? Something from your past? You might be saying - all of the above! I have often asked people when they stopped loving themselves and many can tell me exactly when. I would start there.

Pick just one 10% and "lay that sucker out." With the full lives we lead, how can we possibly fit in ten improvements?

Spend this year working on that one thing. Don't try and deal with the weight, the smoking, the ex, and the aging parents all in one year. That is why we do not stick to improving our 10%s, there are too many to think about. I respect that other "issues" of life are still around, but your main focus should be that one thing. Spend that year doing what you need to do to make it happen – gyms, books, websites, counselling, naturopaths, etc.

I create pockets of time (i.e. turn the TV off!) and make the commitment. I post my resolution everywhere; it becomes my theme for that year. I tell everyone what I am working on so they can keep me accountable. Most importantly, I promise myself, at the end of the year, this one thing will have greatly improved. I will not talk about improving the same thing over and over. I will just do it.

It will change your life to improve this way. I know it is hard. But what are we waiting for? The hardest person to change is the one staring back at you in the mirror.

So now, the next time someone in a grocery store line asks you if you have made any New Year's Resolutions you can say. "Yes, I made ONE and this year I am really going to stick to it."

*"Sometimes the littlest things in life are the hardest to take. You can sit on a mountain more comfortably than on a tack."*
Author Unknown

## This Year's Theme

In addition to my "one thing", I also like to start each year with a theme. It becomes the framework for everything I do. It helps me to focus on the **one thing** I'm going to

work on about me, my approach to work, my home life –
everything is evaluated as to how it works with my theme.
For years, I have been doing this.

Two years ago my theme was "simplify." So I looked at all
areas of my life, home and work, and decided how I could
live my life more .. simply. I focused on my home first and
edited all the closets of everything I did not need. I
looked at my morning and evening routines to make them
simpler so I was not rushing and yelling at Jayda and John
to get out the door for school (ok 90% of the time).

In my business, Sandra and I worked on the processes to
get me out the door to speak and back and how we could
simplify that.

Anytime I would feel, or someone else felt, the need to
add something to my life I would ask, "Does this add to
my theme or not?" I posted the word simplify all over to
remind me.

Last year my theme quickly became "cope." Though I
know that doesn't sound very 90%, it was a very helpful
theme. I had a very full year last year with my husband's,
daughter's and son's health. My special dad had a fall on
the ice and suffered a severe concussion and my beautiful
mom died suddenly. All the while I was called to do what
I do as a motivational speaker. So knowing that a lot of
people needed me to be as full and happy as I can be, I
focused on coping.

What that meant was I did not take on anything that would take away my ability to cope. If I wanted to renovate something or take on a new work project, I would ask myself, "Does this add to my ability to cope or take away from it?" It allowed me to focus solely on what I needed to do to cope most effectively.

This is a much nicer year. My theme for the year is a "fresh start." A major upgrade from the "cope" theme! After coping for so long, I need a new fresh way to live my life. I look at all areas again asking, "How can I do this in a fresh and new way; a way that is centered on being happy and alive?"

I like to look at these themes from a holistic perspective too. How can I add a "fresh start" mentally, physically and spiritually?

Mentally I looked at my work and how I can approach what I do with a fresh start. This is my 19th year as a speaker and I need to look through new eyes and freshen up my work. A fresh new CD and a new website was a great start.

I looked at how I thought about my routines in life, mornings, after school and evenings could be looked at with new eyes. Did I appreciate the routines of life with freshness?

Physically I started taking better care of me. I am very committed to my health and very proud of how I sleep and eat. I eat whole "real" food and nourish me and my family (90% of the time!) but one area that has always been neglected is my cardio health. I am now scheduling in time for me to get out and power walk. Already I feel stronger.

Spiritually I needed a fresh start. I have spent a lot of time praying for help in the past year. This year I want to focus in a fresh new way on gratitude. Anytime I feel overwhelmed with my life I thank God that even though some days seem stressful, it is not layered with coping. I am very grateful for that.

What about you? Do you need a theme this year? If your year is a 90% or a 10% one so far, pick one word or two that you think will add to your life and create a more peaceful year for you. Post that theme on your wall at work and on your mirror at home and just focus on one simple idea. Maybe it is simplify, cope, fresh start, love, care, just breath, be happy. You decide.

*"Start wherever you are and start small."*
Rita Baily

## How do you feel?

*I am on the endless pursuit of what I can do to feel optimum. So I have something left for me and my family at the end of the day. Feeling good is everything. Everything stems from how you feel. Besides, it is really hard to be cranky and be a motivational speaker! I really can't get away with yelling at a cashier. The nature of my work calls me to be a positive person.*

*Motivational speaker Zig Ziglar asks, "If you had a million dollar race horse, would you keep it up half the night giving it booze, cigarettes and junk food?" My guess you would say what I would, "Of course not!" So why wouldn't we take care of ourselves like we would that horse?*

*When you feel good you have a better attitude, you are more patient, loving and understanding towards yourself, and towards your family. Taking care of my health and eating properly has been the key to maintaining a positive attitude. If I feel good ... I act better. Period. And it gives me endless energy that I need to live this very full life.*

*I can't believe the energy, mental clarity and God given spiritual gifts I have gained. 90% of the time in my house we eat my way, 10% of the time we eat Darren's way. (Sounds like a fair ratio to me.) Coming from a farm background Darren thinks each meal has to have meat in it; vegetables have to have cream sauce and two meals a day should end in pie. We had some work to do to meet in the middle.*

*I take handfuls of seaweed, omega oils and supplements. I eat whole food. I drink my water and green tea and indulge in my beloved coffee once in a while. I practice really hard at meditating and quieting my busy mind. I never miss my monthly accupuncture appointment. I would like to know my great, great grandchildren. The only way that will happen is if I take care of myself today.*

*Besides I HAVE to be healthy. Speakers do not get sick days and earned days off. We have to make it to our engagements. I have only had to cancel one engagement due to health (and one due to snowstorm) in 19 years of speaking and I pray that I will never have to do that again.*

*I look at health in a holistic way too. Body, mind and spirit – all three areas are connected. If I am full - mentally, physically and spiritually - I can fill the people around me. If I am depleted, I deplete. I do what I have to do to stay full and happy for me AND my family.*

*Though I believe in our medical system, I do not believe my doctor is responsible for my health. I am responsible for that!*

*What do you need to do to feel your best? To be healthier? Lay that sucker out. I started by choosing one thing I needed to do to be healthy, ie – I quit smoking many, many years ago and I worked on that for the year. Quitting was one thing but eliminating the damage it had done to my body was another. I had to learn to stop the self-sabotage. Then I would choose one unhealthy food a year and eliminate it from our grocery list, white flour, white sugar etc.*

*I have met a lot of people who have had health scares and then made major changes to be healthy. Why do we wait for a scare? Why don't we take care of ourselves now?*

*I believe God whispers at us or he yells. The whispers are the small health concerns. The yells are the large. I prefer to listen to the whispers.*

"To keep the body in good health is a duty... otherwise we shall not be able to keep our mind strong and clear."
Buddha

## My Darren's story

This is my husband Darren's story of not taking care of the 10%s, written by Darren.

My story starts several years ago. In addition to my government job, Darci and I owned two small businesses and had a young family. Our Jayda was three years old and little Johnny was a year old.

Because Darci's speaking career was going so great, I decided to leave my job and become sort of a "Mr. Mom" and help run our two small businesses. I realized a few things during that time: #1-little ones need a lot of care and attention, and #2-small businesses need a lot of care and attention.

Have you ever noticed how when you have a few really big areas in your life, some of the other important parts of your life get neglected? For Darci and I, the areas that we were not receiving enough attention were time for ourselves and time for our marriage. You see, we were really good at being entrepreneurs within our small businesses and really good at being parents to our kids, but we were forgetting to be a husband and wife to each other.

The stress of all we had going on and the disconnect in our marriage was getting to me. Over the course of about a year my mood was getting worse and I was feeling pretty lousy.

Now my Darci is a smart woman, and like most wives, she generally knows I need something before I do! She came to be one day and said, "Darren, I know you are struggling, you just don't seem yourself, we need to change things up. Let's do something fun, let's escape our winter and go to Hawaii!"

We arrive in Waikiki- the biggest tourist area in Hawaii. It is paradise – a beautiful beach next to all kinds of fun restaurants, activities and shopping. Jayda and John were all excited pointing at the palm trees, ice cream shops and the zoo. Darci was excited pointing at all the shoe stores …

I will never forget that first drive into Waikiki. As we drove along, I looked around at all the beauty and at the excitement of my family and I realized that I had everything that I loved all around me and yet, inside I felt … nothing. I wasn't connecting with any of the fun, beauty or happiness. It was a terrible feeling standing on a beach in the middle of paradise and feeling like you should be happy but you're not.

Have you ever had an experience like that? Where you know you should be feeling happy but you just can't connect? As Darci would say, my whispers had turned into yells.

I can honestly say it was one of the weirdest and scariest things I had ever gone through. And so I "laid it out" and began my journey to figure this out and understand how stress, left unchecked, turns into what ever this was.

We returned home and I talked to a lot of doctors and read a lot of books written by doctors. I found out that I was depressed. Since then I have been on a journey of recovery and have tried many different ideas to help me feel my best again. I am happy to say, I've come a long way and learned a great deal.

One of the biggest lessons I have learned is that you can't keep the past bottled up inside or it has a nasty way of coming back and flattening you. Counseling has been extremely helpful in healing some of my past hurts and helping me to feel much better. I also learned a great deal about our bodies natural "good mood fluid", serotonin, and how our diet and lifestyle can help keep our serotonin levels high and make a world of difference in how we feel.

Besides, it is very hard to live with a motivational speaker and not be happy! I am still working on this journey and I can honestly say – it is great to be back. It's nice to be the happy father and husband I used to be.

Hawaii sure looks good now...

*I am proud of Darren for taking action to feel his best. He has learned a lot and helps others to feel their best. Darren now speaks and trains on the topic of stress reduction and the big issues that stress leads to. I am also very grateful for a husband who tries very hard to feel well.*

*I meet people who tell me their husband or wife does not feel well but does not want to do anything about it. When our husband has a sore arm it is easy to take him to a doctor so he can have it fixed. It is a lot harder to fix something you cannot see.*

*Men grow up at dinner tables where they learn to push their feelings aside. They also learn that big boys don't take pills. As I said earlier, maybe your parents were wrong. Maybe it is time to "lay that sucker out" and do something about how you feel.*

*Darren's depression was the ultimate test for me. The test was could I stay full in a depleted situation? Could I have a husband who was depleted some days and yet still come home and be full and happy? I love the saying " There is no testimony without the test."*

*My mom, Beverley, was a breast cancer survivor and she had a poster on her office wall that read ... "If you think money is everything ... you have never been sick."*

## Centurians

I was listening to a radio program and the announcer was interviewing centurians, people who had been lucky enough to live past 100. He asked them the question, "What do you think is the greatest secret to a long life?" Unanimously the group said, "Your ability to deal with stress." They had lived through two wars, dealt with hardships and health concerns but they felt their ability to bounce back determined how long they would live.

I think about that sometimes in a stressful situation. I ask myself, "Am I dealing with this in a way that would insure a long life?"

## Quit cleaning!

I can live in a certain amount of disorder but then I get a bit … goofy when the mess builds and builds. I didn't want to clean all day Saturday; I wanted to be with my family. Even though I was doing a good job of "focusing on the positive 90%" and not trying to be overwhelmed, I was really starting to lose it! Then one day after I was complaining about the mess AGAIN to Darren he said, "I think you have complained about this more than three times … maybe it's time to lay that sucker out." (He thinks he is funny!)

So I did. I got a cleaning service. I feel very blessed to have the money to have this service come in. All I have to say is … what took me so long? Michelle comes in and "shovels" the house out. Michelle is part of my circle of incredible people who make my life easier. I could not keep up with my schedule if it wasn't for her! When people ask me "How do you do it all?" I say … "I don't. I have tons of support."

One of the people who cleaned for us in the past, said, "I love cleaning your house. I feel such results when I leave!" (I appreciate their sense of humor!)

I have a magnet on my fridge that says: "Do Less … Be More." It reminds me of what is really important.

*Pick up the phone book right now and call a cleaning service. Sacrifice a meal out, a new shirt, or something to get this done. Oh and you perfectionists, accept that it will not be the job you can do … and don't clean before they come!*

In addition to a cleaning service everyone needs a really good courier company. I courier everything!! I am a woman who is blessed with a full life, I do not have time to run errands, so I courier as much as I can. In addition to work materials, I also courier personal items. I will literally courier shampoo from the salon and cat food from the veterinarian!

The company I use is owned by a man with a great 90% attitude named Dan. Dan and I have had many conversations over the years and Dan shared something with me his Grandmother always told him.

*"By all means you can have anything you want in your life. Just be sure you know what you have to give up to get it."*

**One huge sucker that many of my audience members say they need to lay out is more time with their families. Balance comes up over and over. Guilt is something parents deal with all the time. How can we learn to have more balance and less guilt? Let's talk about our families now.**

Focus on the 90%

"When you go to sleep at night, you will most likely never regret a single moment of the time you spend with your family."
Author Unknown.

# Your family

*So many people are dealing with guilt and balance issues. I say one of the greatest ways to deal with these challenges is to give the best of you when you are with your family. When we go home and give what is "left over" ... we feel the guilt. Have something left for the people you love at the end of the day.*

*Why do we give 90% to our jobs and only 10% to our families?*

# The Door Knob Theory

I consistently arrive at my engagements friendly, full of energy and excited to be there. Even when I have had to deliver programs sick, on little sleep, or dealing with challenges at home, I never let the client or the audience know, and I always give the best of me.

I would do all this for my client but I would come home and sometimes I would not be the same woman. I would not be the same friendly, full of energy person to my family that I was to my audience. Why not?

My Darren is the nicest man you could ever meet. He is kind, considerate and a wonderful husband and father. I often say if anything every happened to my husband I would never remarry. I could never replace my Darren. I would find someone to cut the grass and build me things and get on with my life. Even during his depression, he always tried and cared about us.

In our house Darren is considered by me and most of the people around us, "the third child." Every day has to hold some fun and adventure for Darren. He is a 10-year-old boy trapped in an adult's body. Darren grew up on a Saskatchewan farm with his two older brothers. On the farm Darren would catch frogs and play for hours with his new found pets. During Darren's depression journey it was especially important that he had an adventure and got out into the sunshine everyday.

While golfing one Saturday, Darren discovered the same kind of frogs that he played with growing up, living in the water beside the golf course. Much to my horror, Darren brought his first set of frogs home for our children to play with ... or should I say, for "all of them" to play with!

When our children were younger, he built a home for the frogs to live in right in our back yard. The frog "sanctuary" as he called it, was built with fiberglass walls and a chicken wire-type top that the neighborhood children could peer in to see our new ... pets. It looked like a see-through compost. We live in the city and we had ... frogs in our yard! Jayda and John and Darren played with the frogs, and when they had all "escaped" they would head out to catch new frogs.

You life is not complete unless you have met our children.

Our daughter Jayda, much like her dad, must go on an adventure every day. Like her mom, she never sits still and never stops talking! She has the greatest laugh and she loves to sing and dance and she LOVES animals (stuffed toy variety or real!) She named her brown frogs "sweetie" and all the green ones were named "Saskatchewan Roughrider." Jayda is pure joy and you cannot help but have fun when you are around her.

Jayda is also the smartest girl I have met. Two years ago on a winter holiday, Jayda picked up an intestinal parasite and we spent months medically and then naturopathically healing her. Through the entire process, I would remind my special girl how brave she was. She would smile and remind me, "I am not brave Mom. I am resilient. Brave would mean I picked this. Resilient means I didn't but I will do what it takes to be well."

Our boy John is named after my dad, two of my grandfathers and Darren's late father. He is a very special boy. I always say, how couldn't he be with a man like his dad to model after? He is quieter than Jayda, but he too loves to go and "do something fun." John loves sports and anything with superheros. All of his frogs were named after superheros. He is a kind, compassionate soul who cares deeply for other people.

You will read later in this book that John is challenged with a weather anxiety. He works very hard at being strong and facing his fears.

When I am away speaking, Darren spends the entire day with our children. Jayda and John call it "Dadderday." A day with Daddy will start like this: Jayda and John wake up. They are in their pajamas. When they were toddlers Darren never changed them out of their pjs. They would walk around all day like that. His theory was … they are going to bed again anyway!

Now they are older, they dress themselves. One of Jayda's teachers said to me, "I can always tell when you are out of town." I was never sure what that meant but good thing I am not a perfectionist!

When Jayda and John were younger my friends would call and say, "I knew it was Darren's day with the kids. I saw them at the park today in their pajamas!" People thought it was cute ... I begged to differ.

As Jayda and John get older the adventures continue. They are always building forts and going on adventures when I am away.

So when I drive and fly home from my engagements, sometimes I am tired and depleted from the travel. I spend the journey home focusing on the 10%s and thinking about the mess the house ... and Jayda and John ... are going to be. Rather than taking the time to focus on the positives of my life, I contradict the message I just spent all day sharing with my audience members, and I focus on the 10%.

When I arrive home, things are exactly as I imagined. There is a small trail of sand from the sandbox (one that's big enough for Darren to fit in!) into our house and backpacks and muddy shoes are by the door. All the couch cushions are off and they have built a fort in the living room.

I look outside and sure enough, my family is in the yard, having a "frogging" good time. When they were young, I would see Jayda and John in their pajamas with lunch still on their faces. I walk out into the yard and the fun's over ... Mommy's home.

Though I know they will help me clean it up later on, because they are very loving and supportive, I felt upset because they didn't do it before I got home. And how come I don't have time to "frog" all day? I line everyone up like a drill sergeant and get everyone cleaning up. Jayda and John both say, "You're not as fun as Daddy!"

Then I lie in bed at night and I feel bad. I had a few precious hours to spend with my family and what did I do? I spent the time focusing on the 10%s rather than the positive 90%s. Why didn't I play? Why didn't I just take a few extra moments when I walked in that door to show my family a positive wife and mother?

I read in a parenting book that we should treat our children and our spouse like we treat our best business client. What courtesy would we extend to them that we do not extend at home? I think if we come home at the end of the day with nothing left for our families, they start to resent our jobs too.

I made a choice. I had had enough of feeling bad about how I greeted my family at the end of a long day. I had enough of being the parent that was not the "fun one."

After complaining about this three times, I laid that sucker out (not Darren, the problem, ha ha). I made a choice. I thought about the fact that if a client called me, no matter what time of day, I would be full of energy for them. Without exception. So how come I could not pull from the same energy place to give my family the best of me?

I sat the three most important people in my life down and told them that I would be the same woman off stage that I am on stage when I am speaking. I will come home and give the best of me because they deserve it. The accountability piece for them was that they needed to chip in more.

So I made a choice. I start by making sure that my drive home is positive. I spend the entire flight or drive home focusing on the positive 90%s rather than the negative 10%s. I call when I am an hour away from home that gives them the time they need to clean up! I take extremely good care of myself when I am on the road, so I am not tired and depleted when I get home.

We came up with "The Door Knob Theory." The idea is that I will not enter that door unless I am in a positive mind set. I put my Focus on the 90% mini-magnifying glass reminder in my car and one on the inside of the garage to remind me to be positive. Sometimes I stand in the garage for 15 minutes praying for strength! But it changes me.

I put my hand on the door knob of the house and I think about my 90%s before I enter: I have a husband who looks after his depression so he can be a fun father to our children, two healthy children (which I will never take for granted again), a house – though middle class – that I would have dreamed of living in as a child, two cars in the garage (and they aren't 1968 Volkswagen beetles), a job I love and my health. I feel that gratitude before I open the door.

I would head out into the yard with a smile on my face to see how many "Saskatchewan Roughriders" they caught that day. I am fully present and there for them. I rarely check messages or emails in the evenings or weekends. When I am off I am off.

Now the challenge is: who is more fun, Mom or Dad? I didn't know how to be fun. I had to learn that. It helps having a fun husband.

Go catch some frogs; it's good for the soul.

*Think about how you can make a choice to make a positive impression when you get home at the end of the day. Implement the Door Knob Theory in your house and do not enter that door until you are positive first. If you find it is a habit to come home unhappy, I ask you Why? When did that start? Lay that out and do some work on that.*

*I meet teenagers who tell me they text their mom or dad to warn him of what mood Mom (or Dad) is in before they get home. Where did we learn it was ok to come home and have nothing left for the people we love?*

*"You don't choose your family. They are God's gift to you, as you are to them."*
Desmond Tutu

## The first 10 minutes

*Did you ever notice that the first ten minutes after you enter the house set the tone for the entire evening? How you enter the house sets the mood. It is very hard to recover once you have blown it – and focused on the 10%s first.*

*If you grew up with a parent where you cleaned the entire kitchen and they came home from work and saw the pot in the sink, you know the impact that had on your own self-esteem. Why would we go home and do what we said we weren't going to repeat from our childhood?*

*I thank Darren for being the man that he is and for being the kind of father who would have that much fun with his children. When Darren was building the frog "sanctuary" a friend was visiting, and she said, "You are so lucky to have a husband who would do that." She is so right.*

*Sure we need to cook dinner, run errands and take children to activities. There are realities of life. But something happens when you just take those first ten minutes to let your family know you are happy to see them and you appreciate them.*

*I can trace every time I have come home, and focused on the 10%, to being depleted myself. I said before, when we are depleted, we deplete. When we are full, we fill. Make sure we are taking care of ourselves enough that we have something left for our families.*

*People tell me we will wake up one day and in a flash, our children will be grown. One day when the mess ends it will be because they have left home. I hear I am going to miss these days...*

## Our children

I play a very major role in my children's self-esteem. Not always focusing on the 10% with them is vital.

It almost becomes a habit to see the 10% with our children – homework, backpacks at the door and their messy rooms. But what about what they do well – their accomplishments? When is the last time we brought attention to their 90%s?

We often learn how to parent our own children from what we learned at the dinner table where we grew up. Maybe some of what we learned was wrong. Maybe we need to reframe some of what we learned and be sure we are giving our children what they need to feel good about themselves. Parenting is the most important job in the world, how much investment do we make in that job? I have met so many people who suffer from low self-esteem. It is so easy to bring our unfinished childhood issues into our role as parents.

When we had our own children, I got a chance to see if the idea of focusing on the positive 90% would help my parenting. I love being a mom; it is truly the best job in the world. When Jayda and John were learning to walk and talk, the parenting books said to encourage them as much as possible. Every time they said a word or stepped a wobbly step, I gave them a ton of positive feedback to encourage them to do more.

As they grew into toddlers, I made sure I took the time to find the positives in this exciting and changing time. There were many challenging days when I thought I would climb the walls, but I made sure that in the midst of it all, I took the time to tell them I loved them, I was proud of them and their accomplishments.

I am not a perfect mother and I have made and I am still making mistakes as I go along. But no matter how the day has gone, and some days are 10%s! I make sure I take the time to lie in my children's beds with them at night and even if we had a rough day, I tell them I love them no matter what.

Now my children are older. I enter a different phase of parenting. I find mornings getting everyone up and out the door to school and evenings back to bed can be stressful times in our house. I don't imagine it is a peaceful to start and end your day with your mom yelling at you! I complained about the lack of peace and cooperation during those times of the day – three times – and then I laid that sucker out. Now we work together to make those times of the day as peaceful as possible – at least 90% of the time.

It goes back to the first "yourself" chapter of this book, if I am full and taking care of me I am more patient and loving. If I am tired and depleted, I deplete and do not handle the stress during those times properly. I really think it starts with me. During our challenging time with Jayda's health and John's anxiety, I had to make sure I wasn't depleted.

I am surrounded by a circle of friends and family who are wonderful parents and I have learned so much from them.

My children are younger. I know, "little people … little problems." People say to me, "Come and talk to me when your Jayda and John are teenagers. We'll see how damn happy you are then!" Ha ha … perhaps I will write a book in those years and let you know how "Focusing on the positive 90%" is working!

Teenagers need to hear positive comments too. Even if their behavior is 10%, they need to know they are loved. Have we told them lately that even though you do not approve of how they are acting, you still love them and you are proud of them? I wasn't the easiest teenager to raise but I always knew for sure that I was loved. A teenager's behavior may be the 10% but there is still a really great kid past the behavior. They need to know they are good.

Another mother told me a story one day about one of her daughter's friends and her mother. This friend was just 15 years old and was pregnant. When someone commented on the situation, this grandmother-to-be said, "It's not what I would have chosen for my daughter but there are worse problems. At least she is healthy. She doesn't have a life-threatening disease. She's not in jail. She is just bringing a blessing into our home a little sooner than we thought she would."

What an inspiration! She had a choice and she choses to support and love her daughter by focusing on the 90% of the situation.

My special mom, Beverley, was only 16 years old when she got pregnant with me. I am grateful for the choices my mom made too.

*"The most important thing I have learned over the years is that there was no way to be a perfect mother and a million ways to be a good one."*
Jill Churchill

**At meal time we go around the table and tell each other a 90% and a 10% of our day. We have taught our children that the world is not perfect but you a have choice on what you focus on. I always say I am a realistic optimist.**

# H.A.L.T.

In addition to mornings and evenings, after school can be a stressful time. Sometimes Jayda and John walk in the door fighting, backpacks get strewn and they are hungry! So rather than focusing on the behaviour, I started to see past it and brought back something I learned from people I know who went through Alcoholics Anonymous (AA). When dealing with depleted, addicted people H.A.L.T., which stands for Hungry, Angry, Lonely and Tired, helps AA and Narcotics Anonymous families cope with their behaviour. I find this very helpful after school.

I make sure I am in a "full" mental state before they arrive home. I take a few minutes to breath and thank

God for my family. I keep my ongoing commitment to being mentally, physically and spiritually happy –"full" so I can fill. It is hard to be a depleted mom meeting depleted kids.

So when they walk in, I am calm and happy. I am so amazed at how my mood becomes the mood of the evening. I am also amazed at how my children mirror to me how I am feeling. If they walk in and are in a bad mood, they go back out, stand at the "doorknob" and calmly re-enter.

I then rule out H - Hungry. Are they hungry? Which they always are. So I have food ready for them. Especially during Jayda's health journey, she was starving.

We then work down the list. Are they A – Angry? Did something happen in the day to upset them? I let them vent without judgement or advice.

Are they L – Lonely? If I was traveling, they missed me and I missed them. Often they just need me to sit beside them letting them talk about their day. Sometimes it is hard for me to just sit when I feel I have so much to do. Then I remember how patiently I listen to clients and audience members.

Finally, are they T – Tired? Yes, they are often tired. I have right brain children that find school very tiring. They need to just "flop out" as John would say and decompress their day. Why would we ask our children to walk in and do homework when we do not want to walk in and do paperwork at the end of our work day?

Once we rule out all letters in H.A.L.T., we could continue on with the evening. Hungry, Angry, Lonely Tired **Mom** meeting Hungry Angry Lonely Tired **Children** will never create a peaceful environment. Remember full...fill; depleted...deplete.

*The other game we like to play is something I learned reading an article in a parenting magazine. It is called "Tell me why I love you." Rather than us telling each other why we love each other we switch that up. It gives Jayda and John a chance to focus on their own positive qualities.*

*"Spending time with your children brings a sense of balance to our lives. It reminds us that the best things in life aren't things."*
Author Unknown

*An audience member, Sherry, shared a story with me that changed what she did to treat her family with more love and respect. She accidentally left the recorder button pushed on their telephone answering machine. For their entire family dinner, their conversation was accidently taped. Later that evening she discovered what had happened. She said she played back that recording and was shocked and embarrassed by how she spoke to her family. She treated them and spoke to them very differently than she would ever speak to a friend or a client.*

*From that day forward she approached her interactions with her spouse and children as if someone where taping her. How proud would she be of what she heard?*

*How proud would we be?*

## Quantity vs Quality

It's not all about quantity as it is quality. Why not make all the errands of life opportunities to be together and to connect. I love to grocery shop on a Tuesday evening. No one is in the store and we grab food to eat for supper as we visit along the way.

Make driving to sports and activities and waiting for games to start times to connect with our children. It doesn't all have to be about board games and focused time. Write notes in their lunches. Send emails and texts telling them you are proud of them. Make everyday bits of time count.

I love dark drives home with Jayda from her piano, voice and dance lessons. They are some of the greatest talks we have.

I was asked in an interview what I thought were the greatest gifts a parent can give their child and my answer was patience, unconditional love and quality time.

## It's never too late

*I don't think it's ever too late. I don't care if your children are 2 years old, 12, 22 or 42 years old; they need to hear positive comments. It is never too late to tell them. Even if you grew up at a dinner table where you did not hear positive, it does not mean you can't learn how to tell your own children. Stop the patterning in your family. If you can say it to your children, they will learn to say it to theirs.*

## Umma

As I said earlier, I try very hard to live with no regrets in my life. I work hard at communicating with the people I love and telling them that I am proud of them and I love them. I learned the importance of that at my dinner table. There will always be 10%s but I work hard at seeing the 90%.

My mom and I never had a perfect relationship. But is any relationship perfect? We had a rough start. My mom got pregnant with me at 16 years old. My dad raised me in the early seventies. My mom remarried twice, had a family of her own and I only saw her on holidays. I always wanted to be closer to my mom but it was like we never knew how to be close. When I was pregnant with our first child I knew I needed to talk to my mom about my feelings. I was 31 years old and I had never had a real meaningful conversation with my mom. I was so worried I would bring some of my unfinished "10%" feelings into my own motherhood role. I really did want to be closer to this woman I felt I hardly knew.

I invited her for a visit and a walk. I was very nervous as we started walking and I told her that my hope for this walk was to be closer to her. I wanted to get to know this woman and hear her side, something I had never heard. We walked for hours. For the first time in my life, I was having a real conversation with my mom. She told me stories of hard it was to leave me, her fears when she lost her leg in a motorcycle accident and her journey with breast cancer. We laughed, we cried, we fought and we bonded. I will never forget that walk.

Shortly after, she sent me a letter saying she would try hard to be my mom, but to be patient because she really didn't know how to be. She wrote she would give as much as she could but didn't know how much that would be. I wrote back promising her that I would try not to have unrealistic expectations. I would meet her where she was at, not where I wished she would be. I would see her through my 90% lens. It was the start of a much closer relationship. It wasn't always easy being her daughter... but sometimes it wasn't easy being my mom either.

Our last summer was the best. I have never felt so close to my mom. Our visits were full of love and laughter. Watching all of her amazing grandchildren in her yard made her the "happiest woman in the world." Her grandchildren all call her "Umma." I never left our visits without a hug, an "I love you" and she ALWAYS said, "You know I am very proud of you right?" I left our last fun summer visit with a bag full of unripe tomatoes from her garden and a feeling like I was finally connecting with my mom like I always prayed I would.

A week after our last summer visit my beautiful mom died suddenly. She was only 59 years old.

There are layers of lessons I could write about. A lesson in communication and how important it is to be brave enough to say what we need to say to those we love. A lesson in expectations. Sometimes we expect a relationship to be how we want it to be; in the meantime, we miss out on all the 90%s. A lesson in forgiveness. I wrote earlier that "My mom taught me forgiveness. Life is too short to carry around the burdens that do not bless your life or the life of others." Every time I came home from our visits this summer I would say "Wow that is the best visit I have ever had." Thank God for those peaceful happy memories.

I went my mom's funeral feeling that nothing was left unsaid. I came home to her unripe tomatoes. My girlfriend said "If I could choose the way I might leave this world and my loved ones, it would be with nothing left unsaid and tomatoes ripening on the counter."

I know first hand it is hard to have those difficult conversations with those you love. Live no regrets. Be brave. Even if they don't respond the way you want them to... or at all... know that you tried. See those you love through your 90% magnifying glass. You will never regret that.

*"The bitterest tears shed over graves are for words left unsaid and deeds left undone."*
Harriet Beecher Stowe

*Create 90% lists of all the things you love about the people that you care about and share it with them. Don't wait to share it in their eulogy.*

# John

A young man named John emailed me and his email read:

*"Hello Darci, my name is John. This morning I woke up and there was this small magnifying glass – "Focus on the 90%" – sitting on the kitchen table. My mom was at your presentation last night and she taped a note onto your magnifying glass and it said, "John, I was at a presentation last night for work and the woman talking gave us this magnifying glass to take home. She told us it was never too late to tell your children you love them. So John I want you to know … I love you and I am very proud of you."*

*John then went on to write. "Thank you for doing that Darci as I am 18 years old and my mom has never told me that before."*

**If you don't know how to say the words, write them down. Send a card, write an email or send a text! It is never too late …**

# Margaret

*"Darci my name is Margaret and I was in the front row of your presentation yesterday. Two things you said hit me hard.*

*The first thing was you reminded me I have a role to play in my son's self-esteem. My son has suffered from low self-esteem his whole life. The second thing was ... I sat there thinking that my son is 28 years old and I needed to tell him I love him and I am proud of him. I never heard anything positive growing up and I have always wondered how I would tell my boy what I did not hear.*

*So after your presentation I drove right to his apartment and when he opened the door I gave him a big hug and said, "I love you." I could tell he was quite shocked. He pulled away from my hug and asked me, "Mom – are you dying or something?"*

Ha ha ...

**Do you need to put a message on a post it note, send an email or drive to someone's house and deliver a hug?**

## Our spouses

## If I can't do anything right ... I won't do anything at all.

Like many husbands, my Darren needs a lot of positive feedback. Many of us have really great husbands and we forget to tell them how much we appreciate them. They need to hear they are good. I learned this very early in our marriage. Focusing on Darren's 90% is a way to keep his self-esteem (and his housework motivation) high.

However I found for the first few years of our marriage that when Darren tried to help me around the house it was never quite ... good enough. It wasn't up to my "standard." (Those were the days before children so I actually had a standard.)

He rolls towels and jams them in the linen closet. His idea of making the bed is just pulling up the bedspread, sheets all bunched underneath. Or worse, he doesn't make a bed because ... his theory is: we're going to bed again anyway!

I used to do a lot of nagging about this silly 10% stuff when one day Darren said, "You know when you make me feel like I can't do anything right, I don't want to do anything at all."

I decided to practice my own message. I would focus on the positive 90% instead of the negative 10%. Rolled up towels are still clean, so I stopped refolding them.

I still slip sometimes and nag about something not being good enough but when I do, Darren says with a sweet smile (and a touch of sarcasm) "quite the motivational speaker."

I know I have a role to play in Darren's self-esteem and motivation. Nagging him does not make him, or me, feel good. That is not the wife I wanted to be. Darren is not perfect but neither am I. He has his fair share of 10%s that bug and annoy me but he would tell you ... and I would have to agree ... I am not always easy to live with either.

Darren is a really great man. I focus on his 90%s and he treats me and our children with love and respect. All I need to do is watch how some husbands treat their wives in a store line up to realize how lucky I am.

An audience member said to me, "Instead of trying to make my husband a better husband, I decided to make me a better wife."

I can trace the times I have nagged Darren to being depleted. The more I take care of myself, the fuller I am, the more I enter the marriage full and not depleted.

The more I feel better about myself the less I find fault in him.

Darren and I need to work on our marriage. We learned a lot during the time our children were younger about what happens when we don't take time for each other. We arrange weekly dates – even for an hour walk – to reconnect. We also like to read marriage books for other great ideas.

One of the best marriage book we have read is called "Five Love Languages" by Dr. Gary Chapman. It has changed how we focus on each other.

Gary in his book explains that we all have a "love language" that makes us feel special. Mine is "acts of service" and Darren's is "physical touch." So when Darren does an "act of service" for me like cleaning the house or my car or cutting the grass, etc., I feel very loved. But if I take the time to clean his car and the house, he barely notices because that is not his language. However, if I actually sit beside him and watch a movie or hold his hand while we go for a walk, he feels loved. We have learned and are committing to each other's language.

*Create a 90% list of your spouse/partner and share it with them. When you find yourself focusing on their 10%s, take out your list and read it. It will remind you of all their 90%s.*

## The Trouble Tree

Our wonderful priest, Father Steve shared this story in his sermon.

*The carpenter I had just hired to help me restore an old farmhouse had just finished a rough first day on the job. A flat tire made him lose an hour of work, his electric saw quit and now his ancient pickup truck refused to start.*

*While I drove him home, he sat in stone silence. On arriving he invited me in to meet his family. As we walked toward the front door, he paused briefly at a small tree, touching the tips of the branches with both hands. When opening the door, he underwent an amazing transformation. His tanned face was smiling as he hugged his two small children and gave his wife a kiss.*

*Afterward he walked me to the car. We passed the tree and my curiosity got the better of me. I asked him about what I had seen him do earlier.*

*"Oh, that's my trouble tree," he replied. "I know I can't help having troubles on the job, but one thing's for sure, troubles don't belong in the house with my wife and children. So I just hang them up on the tree every night and when I come home. Then in the morning I pick them again."*

*"Funny thing is," he smiled, "when I come out in the morning to pick them up, there ain't nearly as many as I remember hanging up the night before."*

## Speaking of trees ...

My dad was right, the older you get, the faster time goes by. Some years I feel like I just put the Christmas decorations away and I am taking them out again. Well maybe that is because they are unpacked so early in our house. Darren, my husband, aka the "third child" ... loves Christmas and likes to put the Christmas tree up November 1st. He likes to go from Halloween straight into Christmas!

As if that isn't weird enough ... he never likes to take it down ... mid January works for him ... mid January?? By then I could take a flame-thrower to it all! (That wasn't very positive was it?)

So for the first few years of marriage I thought this was really ridiculous. But you know as the years have gone by I have learned to "Focus on the 90%" of it all and I have learned to love it too ... ok ... appreciate it. I've tried to have this attitude about the rest of the season as well. Darren's memory of his beloved mom at Christmas time was her running around, stressed, tired and over worked. Trying to make everything perfect for everyone else. I remember the first Christmas after she passed away. I was frantically running around the house vacuum in hand, baking dishes heaped in the sink – definitely focusing on the 10%! Then I noticed Dottie's picture smiling back at me. I could just hear her saying to me, "Slow down Darci. You know how fast time goes. Focus on what really matters." From that moment on, I made a decision to check out of the Christmas "rat race" and enjoy the true reason for the season.

I want to be an example to my children of what Christmas means. I want their memory of me at Christmas to be a positive one. Besides, I have "Mr. Fun Dad" to compete with!

So when I catch myself getting overwhelmed, I stop and ask myself, "Have I complained three times about this and how can I eliminate this stress?" I "lay that sucker out." We need to learn to make it more peaceful. I buy my baking from a special Christian woman in our neighborhood and I let Jayda and John wrap all the presents (however they like).

We stopped buying for all the adults and donate the money to a much-needed charity. I leave the tree decorating to Jayda and John. We eat meals on a picnic blanket beside the tree because the kids love it. I really try and discipline myself to enjoy it. Just slow down and enjoy the true reason for the season.

Shucks … I guess I'll have to retire my flame-thrower.

# Choice

On an airplane, I sat with a man who had a job that took him out of town for extended periods of time. I asked him if his family would be at the airport to pick him up. He exclaimed, "No – me coming home is not their 90%." and he walked off the plane. I sat there wondering why and wondering when he would make some choices to change that?

It really is about choices. I have a colleague whose husband works out of town. He is away from home three weeks of the month working, and home with his family for one week. Her children are similar in age to mine and I asked her, "How do you do it?" She said to me, "When Mike is away he is away. When he is home, he is home. When Mike is home for his week with us, he is here for us. He is the best father and husband because he knows the time is short and precious."

Perhaps Mike would rather be with his buddies at happy hour when he gets home, but he makes a choice. I am sure it isn't easy some days but his family feels loved and cared for, with less guilt. It is about quality time, not quantity.

*"Don't marry the person you think you can live with; marry only the individual you think you can't live without."*
James C. Dobson

*I really admire former Toronto Argonaut, Michael "Pinball" Clemons. I have seen him speak and he has a powerful message. Interviewed in a Canadian Family Magazine article I like what he had to say about family:*

*"One of the best things you can do for your children is be a living example; to treat their mother with dignity, love and respect. And to truly love your child, you should treat them as special and unique."*

*I admire his integrity, on and off the field (even though he is not a Saskatchewan Roughrider ...)*

It is great to say that you want to be a better family member, spouse and parent but exactly what do we need to DO to be that person?

It is easy to put our hand on the doorknob and say, "I will walk in this house today and be a better parent" but

HOW? What steps need to be taken, what words need to be said, what patience needs to be shown?

When people at the end of my workshops say, "Thank you I will leave your presentation today and go home and be a better husband and father."

I always say, "That is wonderful, but HOW will you do that?"

*When I am interviewed I am often asked the same question, "How do you achieve balance with your schedule?" I am ruthless when it comes to balance. There are many ways I keep a balance in my life and I have mentioned some in this book. I am happy with what I have and I have an incredible support system in place. When I am not working, I am not working.*

*Our jobs can impact how we treat our families. It is important that we carry the same positive 90% magnifying glass back to our workplaces as well. I love my job, but I remember my job is simply that ... my job. It does not completely define me. Being a speaker is just one role that I play in my life. What I focus on in that job determines what I have left for my family at the end of the day.*

*I think it is ridiculous that we grow up in a society where we learn that we give the best of ourselves to our work and then come home with nothing left for our families. Maybe we learned that at our dinner table as children growing up and it is time to do it differently.*

*Our spouses get really tired of hearing about our day. They get tired of us coming home tired and complaining about work.*

*I remember when our son John accidentally picked up the business line in our home and spoke to a client of mine. I actually yelled at our special boy for doing that. It took me a few minutes before I realized had made a mistake. I sat my Jayda and John down and I apologized to my boy and I told them both I never want them to think that my job is more important than they are.*

*I tell my children that despite any success my career brings me there is no place I would rather be than home with them.*

*Let's talk about your job.*

Focus on the 90%

*"Never continue in a job you don't enjoy. If you're happy in what you're doing, you'll like yourself, you'll have inner peace. And if you have that you will have had more success than you could possibly have imagined."*
Johnny Carson

# Your Job

*Have you ever met anyone who complains about their job? Maybe you live with them? We all have at least 10% negative at our job – sometimes it seems like more. When we go to work with our magnifying glass on the 10% of our job the ripple effect is huge. It first affects how we do our job because it is difficult to be enthusiastic about something we don't enjoy.*

*Then our negative attitude ripples out to our co-workers because it is not easy to work with someone who is complaining all the time. How can we build a "team" with people who drag themselves to work? Can't you tell when someone is focused on the 10%? People will often say to me "I am JUST A _____." How can you feel good about your job when you have already defined yourself that way?*

*Then the ripple effect extends to our clients and the service we provide to them. It is very difficult to provide great service if you have a poor attitude. When clients call me to share my 90% message with their staff they sometimes say that they are having issues with low morale and poor service delivery. I always say the same thing to them, "You must have people in your organization who don't enjoy their job any more." Sure enough, when I speak to the staff ahead of time, it is true. Some have moved their magnifying glass to the 10% and we have all been served by someone who does not want to be there.*

*The ripple effect of a negative attitude at work not only affects our work performance, those we work with and our clients, it also affects us personally. It affects our self-esteem because many people tie their self-esteem to their job. Doing something you do not enjoy or do not feel is of value is very hard on you.*

*The ripple effect does not end there. It also affects our families. When we have a negative attitude at work we tend to bring that home and our family suffers every evening at the dinner table. They hear about how much we dislike what we do. It affects our children as they listen to us talk about our jobs at the end of the day. We teach them that the job - that provides for the family - is not a place you should go to and enjoy. We start a whole new generation of future workers at our dinner table - a generation that is learning that where you will work will not make you happy.*

*I am not sure what our Jayda and John will do for a career someday (though I suspect Jayda will care for animals and John will care for people). I already tell them to do something you enjoy.*

I think it is important to step outside of our job once in a while and view it through a 90% lens. Literally take a mental step away from it and ask, "What is still good, why do I stay, etc.?" Observe it from a different angle. Sometimes we are so caught up in the stress, we forget to see what is still 90%. The reasons we wanted the job in the first place.

As you read earlier, I like to interview a portion of my audience before I speak to them. You can imagine how interesting is for me to hear from people I have never met before. These people share their 90%s and their 10%s of their job with me, a complete stranger.

In one day, I can get an email from two employees from the same company, with the same job and the same pay but I receive two completely different impressions of their job. One is a happy 90% employee and the other one is the unhappy 10%.

I have spent years formally and informally "researching" what separates these two people. When I meet the people who complain the most, I leave the seminar wondering if it is the job or are they just not happy and work is the place where everyone else has to suffer for their unhappiness?

There is a very interesting connection between the happiest and the unhappiest people I meet. They have both learned about work at their two different dinner tables growing up.

It might be the same for you. If you grew up with 90% parents who enjoyed their work, you grew up with a framework, a belief system about work. You grew up believing that your work should be a place that you go to that makes you happy. Maybe you learned that if you didn't enjoy it, you should never stay in that job. When I speak to nurses or teachers, I ask them to raise their hand if they had a parent who was also a nurse or a teacher. Many hands go up in the air.

However, if you grew up with 10% parents who complained about their job, you are more likely today to be someone who does the same. You learned a belief system that where you work will not make you happy. It is simply a place you go to provide for your family, a means to an end. If you scattered when Dad got home from work because he was tired and angry, then chances are, you learned to do what you thought was right. The people I know who complain the most about their jobs are the ones who grew up with "half empty" parents who did the same.

Maybe what you learned at the table about what work should represent in your life was wrong? Maybe work is a place that should make you happy? Your job should be an extension of your happy life, not a place you go to be unhappy. I am positive we were not put on this earth to work, be unhappy and then die! I know people who believe that once they put in 30 good years with a company, they will get a nice gold watch and then they will be happy! Yikes, I think we should try and be happy along the way.

People will come up to me after a presentation and say, "You need to come and talk to my husband/wife – all they do is come home at the end of the day and complain."

Why would they do that?

I received this email from Rick:

*My wife always says to me "If you hate your job so much, why don't you quit?" I asked her "Why do you think I hate my job?" She said, "Because you come home every night and complain." I replied, "I don't hate my job at all; actually I really like what I do." She asked, "Then why do you complain?"*

*Darci my honest answer to her was "I don't know."*

*I got the answer in your presentation today. I complain about my job because it is a habit. I listened to my own father complain every night about his job and I listen to my coworkers in the staff room do the same. I am going to "lay that sucker out" and start appreciating my job. Maybe it is time to reframe what I learned at the dinner table. No wonder my own children complain about where they work! They have learned that from me."*

Many of the people I know in my life who complain about their job, actually really enjoy what they do and wouldn't dream of doing something else. So when I say to my friend, "Why do you complain then?" My friend said to me, "I don't know, it's just what we do!"

Complaining is truly a habit. What if we broke the habit and were grateful for our work?

*"My father taught me to work; he did not teach me to love it."*
William Adams

# Janet

I was invited to speak at a Teachers' Professional Development Day (PD Day). My job was to pump up the teachers before they started the new school year. I was to spend the morning reminding them of the unbelievable importance of their job and how their attitude at work affects everyone they work with, and most importantly, every student they teach.

I have been fortunate to speak at many PD Days and when I asked a teacher in one of my presentations what teaching was like she said, "I am social worker, referee, psychologist, politician, doctor, nurse, entertainer, nutritionist and coach." I think next to parenting, teaching is the most important job in the world. Our children are blessed to have been taught by some amazing 90% teachers.

The first to arrive at the PD Day was a young woman who sat at the front table. No one arrives at a training session first and sits in the front. Most people who arrive early sit in the back and the late people sit up front. Kind of like church. She fanned out a selection of colored highlighters, positioned her bottle of water and her Chapstick on the table in front of her. She then hung a sweater on the back of her chair. She was READY for her training session!

This enthusiastic woman sat right up front with a great smile the entire time I talked. She sat on the edge of her seat and hung on every word I said. She made copious notes (and highlighted many points!) and shared at every workshop opportunity. She was a light in the room. At the break she rushed up to me and said, "You are the greatest speaker I have ever seen!" Then she admitted, "Well, you are the only speaker I have ever seen!" I laughed and asked how she kept herself so positive.

She introduced herself as Janet and explained to me that this was her first year of teaching. I went and visited her classroom, all decorated with flowers, bees and happy faces. I wished her well and I said a prayer on the way home that she would keep that enthusiasm for her important job. My guess was she grew up at the dinner table with incredible parents.

A year later I was shopping in a retail store with my very energetic children. The woman helping me seemed very familiar. She was a very friendly and enthusiastic sales associate with a great smile, who ran around the store and played peek-a-boo with Jayda and John while I tried clothes on.

When I looked at her name tag, it hit me – it was Janet, the teacher from the Professional Development Day! I said, "Aren't you the teacher I met last year?" She responded "Yes I am! You're the magnifying glass lady ... I knew I recognized you!" I asked her what she was doing working in a retail store. What happened to her teaching career?

She replied, "I taught for a year and I hated it. So I quit." I responded, "Good for you, it takes courage quit something you don't want to do." She said with a smile, "That isn't what my parents had to say about it. They paid for my education."

She went on to explain that she had worked retail during university and thought she could better serve people in a job she enjoyed. Even in her first year she knew teaching was not for her. She said she had seen far too many friends stay in jobs that did not make them happy.

As I was leaving with Jayda and John I stopped on the way out, turned around and said, "Janet, thank you. Thank you for not teaching my children and their children with an attitude that shows you don't want to be there for the next 35 years of your life."

*"The decisions you make about your work life are especially important, since most people spend more of their waking lives working than doing anything else. Your choices will affect, not only yourself and those closest to you, but in some way the whole world."*
Laurence G. Boldt

## Greatest Impact

I love one-on-one time with our children. I find the focused one-on-one time to be a real "fill" for us. I like to unplug technology whenever I can and just sit and "be."

One morning, I had a gift of time with John. There is nothing better than spending time alone with the nicest boy I know. John and I woke up before anyone else and he wanted to play a game called "The Family Dinner Box of Questions." It is a deck of cards that asks unique questions to get dialogue going around the dinner table. We love playing it and hearing about "What wild animal would you keep for a pet?", "Using one word, how would you describe your family?", etc.

The question on my card to John was, "What teacher has had the greatest impact on your life?" Without a second of hesitation he said, "Ms.Merk." He went on to explain in great detail how supported he has felt and what a friend she has been to him when he really needed one. He told me "I will never forget her mom and all she has done for me."

Our son, John is dealing with a weather anxiety. During a big thunder storm a while back, it's like a switch flipped. Since then he has not wanted to go outside if it's cloudy, for fear it will turn into a bad weather day. If it was raining, he did not want to go to school. Needless to say, it added a 10% stress to our morning routine! John sees a counselor which is helping but he was still so fearful of

"What if it rains once I get to school?" that I called John's teacher and explained our situation. She said in her calm way, "No problem, I'll just let John stay in at recess if he is feeling stressed."

In one call, she took away a huge challenge for us. Whenever John would feel stressed in the morning, I would say, "No worries John, remember what Ms. Merk said. You can stay in if you need to." He would take a deep breath and off to school he would go.

Her choice to be patient and loving added a 90% to a 10% situation. I am so grateful for her.

*"Loving-kindness and compassion are the basis for wise, powerful, sometimes gentle, and sometimes fierce actions that can really make a difference – in our own lives and those of others."*
Sharon Salzberg

***Take a few minutes and think about the people who make/made a difference in your life. Whose life do you make a difference in?***

## Making a Difference

Though we have worked hard with John, he entered another year with the same weather concern. We were blessed again with another wonderful teacher.

I have spoken to thousands of teachers and I ask them to share with me the reason they chose teaching as a career. Most would say, "To make a difference in the lives of their students." Cindy made a huge difference to John.

John and I wanted to share with you the letter he wrote to Cindy to thank her for this year.

Dear mrs. Welburn you are a very special teacher and I can't believe I am saying this but iam a little upset that the year ended so qwickly, Well anyway thank you sooooooooooooooooooooooooo Much for letting me stay in for recess. My year would of Been a lot different if not. thanks so mush you will neverBe forgoten never ever never ever never ever.

LOVE
John

I hope it is a reminder to all of us that we all have choice in who we serve for a living. If stay focused on the 90%s of why we wanted the job in the first place, we then make the difference we thought we would.

*"We make a living by what we get, but we make a life by what we give."*
Winston Churchill

## Something Great

When John asked me the question "Mom, which teacher has had the greatest impact on you?" I too did not hesitate when I said, "Mr. Majors."

I went on to tell him the story of Mr. Majors, my Grade 12 Chemistry teacher. I did not like chemistry. It's not that I didn't like chemistry – I didn't like school. It was not a 90% for me. I really struggled at school. I did not like to sit all day, I loved to talk (go figure) and I would challenge my teachers all the time. I would ask my teachers why I needed to memorize the names of lakes, I refused to dissect the frog because I thought it was gross, and on and on. I skipped a lot (which could help explain why my grades suffered) and I couldn't wait to graduate.

Chemistry was by far my greatest challenge. My constant questions to Mr. Majors were, "Why do I need to know this?" and "When will I ever use this in my life?" My first semester I received a mark of 16%. Yup 16%.

My year-end chemistry mark would determine if I was to graduate. I had my 1968 Volkswagen packed and I was ready to live my life. I knew I had to get serious about this class. I asked Mr. Majors if he would help me. I promised him I would show up if he would please give me a little extra help. He agreed. We worked hard together. He didn't give up on me.

The last day of school when they were passing out report cards. I learned that Mr. Majors had mine and I was to go and see him after school. I thought the worst.

There he was at his desk. I could see the brown envelope. He looked up and said "Oh good I wanted to talk to you." I could smell summer school in the air.

He held out my report card and I asked him in a quiet nervous voice "Did I pass?" He let me open the envelope and whew ... I had passed.

He walked me out of his classroom and as I was walking down the hall to 'freedom' he said, "I want to tell you something." My heart sank. What else??

He said, "Darci, I don't know where you are going in that '68 beetle or where life will take you but I know a couple of things. I know for sure that whatever you go on and do in your life, it will have absolutely NOTHING to do with chemistry.

And I know something else, that whatever you go on to do in your life, it will be something great." And he turned and walked away.

I think about Mr. Majors and his parting words all the time. I think they have had an impact on who I've become today.

***How often do we tell people around us they are great?***

*"Too often we underestimate the power of a touch, a smile, a kind word, a listening ear, an honest compliment, or the smallest act of caring, all of which have the potential to turn a life around."*
Leo Buscaglia

## Richard

Sitting at the front table at one of my presentations was a young man named Richard. He looked unhappy. As I spoke, he gave very little feedback. He just seemed to be in his own world. He left my training day and didn't say goodbye to anyone. Just got up and walked out. I prayed he was okay.

The next day I received an email from Richard. Since he seemed so unhappy in the presentation I thought he would be emailing to complain about something. His email read:

*"Hi Darci. My name is Richard. I was the guy who sat up front yesterday. You might have noticed I didn't want to be there. I didn't want some consultant telling me how to do my job. Minutes into your presentation I knew it would be different. You really struck a chord with me. I sat there listening to you and I realized ... I hate this job. I have worked here for seven years and there is not a day I do not wake up and push the snooze bar fifteen times, dreading coming to this place. It is not at all what I wanted to do with my life. I complain at work and at home constantly about what I do. In my selfishness I never realized the impact my attitude must have on my coworkers. Sitting around the staff room listening to me complain about this job must be exhausting for them. I realized what an impact that must have on the service I deliver to my clients. No wonder I never meet my sales goals.*

*"What really hit me Darci, was when you spoke about the personal areas of our life. It does affect my self-esteem doing a job I do not enjoy. I have changed. I used to be a nicer person. I have a tremendous wife and two great kids. I can't remember the last time I did not walk through the door tired and pushing my kids aside. I can't remember a meal I have*

*eaten with my family that I have not spent time complaining about my day.*

*"I went home last night and I told my family I was sorry for doing that all these years. My wife and I sat up half the night talking and we decided we needed to make some changes.*

*"So Darci, I wanted to let you know, I "laid that sucker out." I walked into my boss's office this morning and I quit my job. And I told him ... it was because of you."*

Yikes! That wasn't quite what I had meant, but I emailed Richard back and told him he should be proud of himself. It takes courage to quit. I wished him well in whatever his next venture was to be.

A few emails up from Richard's was an email from his manager. The subject line of his email read: *"Thank you."* The body of his email read: *"Thank you Darci for helping me to get rid of someone who has been very unhappy in our company for many years."*

***How do you feel about your job? A good gauge is to ask yourself this: When someone asks you about your job, what do you say? What is the first thing you talk about, the positive 90% or the 10%? When someone at a BBQ asks you what you do, what do you say? What do you say in the staff room? At your own dinner table? What are your children hearing?***

*"Work is either fun or drudgery. It depends on your attitude. I like fun."*
Colleen C. Barrett

Have you ever known anyone who left a job for one that paid less money, in order to be happy?

I love cab drivers – they have such interesting life stories. Bernie the cab driver told me why he left his previous job to drive cab. The stress and pressure of his last job were getting the best of him. He said driving that cab, he didn't make the money he used to but now he had a lot less stress and he has his health and his marriage back.

CHANGE seems to be a the biggest stress for many of my audiences in their jobs. The thing about change is, it is always going to happen. I think how we view change started at our dinner table, too. If we view it as something that will allow the company and us to grow and evolve, we are more likely to embrace it as "what happens." If we learned it was bad, and management, the union or the board are just out to get us...we are less likely to cope with the changes.

Change is inevitable for the rest of creation, we will always have change in our job. How do you view it??

*We all have a choice about what we focus on at work. We choose the job we have. We can also choose the attitude we bring to our job.*

*So if your choice is to stay in your job for whatever reason, how can you stay focused on the positive 90%? No job is perfect. The grass is not always greener at another job. The challenge is to find the positives in whatever it is we choose to do for a living.*

*One way I have found very successful for many of my clients is to stay focused on why you ever wanted this job in the first place. Stay focused on the meaning of the job or the difference you make in the job you do.*

## The Difference

I was sitting in a waiting room at a doctor's office. I love waiting in waiting rooms. It is my chance to sit, do nothing and read a magazine. I am always so annoyed when they call my name as I am always half way through a great article!

While I was waiting, a Paratransit van pulled up. I could see out the window into the parking lot and I watched as the driver of this Paratransit vehicle jumped out and ran enthusiastically to the side door to help his customer. He helped out an elderly man in his wheelchair. The elderly man was dressed in a sharp three-piece suit, shoes shined to a perfect polish and hat on his head. He reminded me of my late grandfather, "Pop."

The driver pushed the wheelchair to the employee behind the counter and announced in a loud voice, "Excuse me. Mr. Wright is here to see you." He turned to Mr. Wright, put his right hand to his forehead, stood tall and gave him a military salute. He said, "Sergeant Major Sir, I will be back in an hour to pick you up."

He ran past us in the waiting room, jumped in his vehicle and was gone. Ten minutes later he returned. As he pulled up I put my magazine down to watch his "encore" performance. The driver again jumped out and ran to the side of his van. He opened the doors with care and helped out an elderly woman in her wheelchair. She looked to be about 101 years old. She was dressed in a floral dress, hat on her head, her gloved hands clutching her purse on her lap.

The driver laughed and chatted with her as he wheeled her past the waiting area. Once again he approached the receptionist and announced with respect in his voice, "Excuse me. Mrs. Beachwood is here for her appointment." He treated his passenger as if royalty had arrived. He got down on one knee, knelt beside her wheelchair and took her frail gloved hand in his. He kissed her hand and said "Gorgeous, I'll be back in an hour to pick you up."

He ran past us again and left her sitting in her chair beaming. He left all of us in the waiting room tearing up! All I could think of as he climbed back in his driver's seat was that this was someone who obviously makes a choice to find the positives in what he chooses to do for a living.

He must understand that for many of his customers he may be one of the few people they see in a week. For some he may be like family. For Mr. Wright and Mrs. Beachwood, he makes a choice to brighten their day. If he dragged himself to work only seeing the 10%, how would that affect his attitude towards what he does and the very special people he serves?

I am sure his job is not perfect, without 10%s. I am sure some days he does not feel like picking people up and I am sure not all of his customers are as friendly as Mr. Wright and Mrs. Beachwood. He makes a choice. His choice is that he will stay focused on the positive 90%. The difference he makes. Just like the teachers in my boy John's life.

*"It's easy to make a buck. It's a lot tougher to make a difference."*
Tom Brokaw

# Mary

I am on the endless pursuit to find people who are happy in their jobs. People who are proud of what they do and can Focus on their 90%s.

One of the happiest women I have met is a hotel employee named "Mary." We checked into the hotel and I decided I would go and set up the banquet room while Darren took our Jayda and John swimming in the hotel pool.

I entered the banquet room and there – singing to herself – was a kind-looking woman, dressed in a black and white uniform. I introduced myself as the speaker for tomorrow's conference and she introduced herself as Mary. A fitting name I thought, as you could tell she was a loving soul. She set up the tables as I set out my materials. We chatted like we had known each other for years. She is one of those people who makes you feel special and you can't help but like her.

Mary called herself the "Jacqueline of all trades" at the hotel and told me she had worked at the hotel "since dinosaurs had roamed the earth." She was in charge of the banquet area and she also cleaned the hotel rooms for the guests. She shared with me how much she loved her job and she told me part of her job was to bring joy to all her guests.

I noticed on the menu for the next day there would be a desert with gooseberries on the side. I remarked to Mary how my husband Darren had grown up on a Saskatchewan farm with gooseberry bushes and how much he and our children loved them. I thanked her for our visit and went to join my family.

You can tell the attitude of the hotel staff by how they clean your room. I have stayed in many hotels where some of the staff put our children's special blankets and toys on the floor! Not Mary, she did something special.

She folded Jayda and John's blankets into swan shapes on the beds.

She arranged all of John's superhero action figures in a fighting position on the dresser.

She linked the arms of Jayda's stuffed animal frogs together in a big circle on the bed. She then carefully tucked a gooseberry in each one of their folded arms.

As we looked around that room in amazement, I stood there thinking that this special woman in that dusty prairie hotel might actually have the meaning of life figured out. She is happy and definitely brought joy to us.

*"There are those who give with joy, and that joy is their reward."*
Kahlil Gibran

**Make a 90% list of why you wanted the job in the first place. Make a 10% list. If your 10% outweighs your 90% list, is it time to move on?**

# I can't just quit!

Some of you are reading this and saying, "I can't just quit my job!" I understand that. If that is your situation, is there some way you can make going to work more enjoyable?

Even my awesome job has it's 10%s. No sick days, lost luggage, "not so great" hotel rooms just to name a few. I have to make it no matter what. I have travelled all night and I have even slept in my van! Have you ever seen the "Saturday Night Live" skit with Chris Farley playing motivational speaker, Matt Foley, a speaker who lived in his van by the river? I could relate that day!!

To help me focus on what is really important I have put a glass top on my desk. Under that glass, I have pictures of my family and many of the pictures my children have drawn for me. If I am having a bad day, I just look at what is really important to me. The reason I am doing the work in the first place. It grounds me to what is important.

If you have been complaining about the same problems at work for more than three times, maybe it is time to "lay that sucker out" and ask yourself what you can control and what you can't?

I will often do a workshop in my presentations where I will have the group lay out their 10%s – what they do not enjoy about their jobs – on flip chart pages. Once all of them are written down we go back and look at the list. We circle which of their complaints they have control over and which they don't.

Workshop after workshop so many people circle things that they just can't control. In the end there is only one or two concerns that they have direct control over. So my next question is, "What are you going to do about it?" If you can't control it, why complain about it? If you can control it, why not do something about it?

Maybe there are 90%s in the job that you have forgotten about. What if you approached the job with the attitude that if it's not time to leave, there must be something the job still has to teach you? Find out what that is.

At one of my presentations, there were cookies left over from the break. My client said to me, "If you want to take a couple of cookies home for your kids, help yourself." Since this would be a huge treat in our house, I took her up on her offer and walked over to the cookie table. There were two employees already there; one with a bag and the other scooping the cookies into it. I overheard them saying, "It is the least they can do, buying us cookies. They owe us."

Needless to say I did not take a cookie home and I left wondering what and where they had learned about entitlement.

Maybe just trying to be grateful for your job will help you see it as a positive. Being employed is a blessing in itself. I have met a lot of people who are unemployed and would be grateful to have any job.

In one of my presentations a beautiful woman stood up and in her broken English she said with passion, "You should all kiss the ground you walk on. You are lucky to be alive, to live in a country where you have choices where you can go to work. You are all safe in this building today, you did not have to fear gathering as a group. Where I am from there is fear everyday and no work for anyone. I am very grateful for this work and you all should be too." As she sat down, you could have heard a pin drop.

The author Amy Tan said: *"If you can't change your fate, change your attitude."*

Maybe it's time to do just that.

**Sometimes we stay in a job that slowly wears away at us. I had a woman tell me, "My job hurts my soul." I told her she had to leave. No job is worth your stress, your peace of mind, your family and certainly not your soul.**

## Here I go again on my own...

No job I have ever had has been 100% perfect. They all have their 10%s.

My first job was working for my dad in his Volkswagen repair shop in the back yard of our home. It was not an easy job, scrubbing parts, changing oil, and setting valves on the Beetles. One of the 90%s were the long talks Dad and I would have around the workbench.

Years later, I went to work as a bus girl in a restaurant and then worked in the retail industry in high school. We should all have to work in a garage, wait tables or work retail at least once in our lives for a reality lesson! The most grateful employees I meet are ones that have worked elsewhere. Ones that have done a previous job that they did not want to do again. They appreciate what they have because they know what the alternative looks like.

When I was 18 years old, I packed up my 1968 Volkswagen Beetle (rebuilt by Dad and I) and as I headed off down the highway, I popped in my "Whitesnake" cassette tape.

I arrived in a new city to live in my Aunt Susan's basement while I looked for a summer job. My aunt – my dad's sister – is a very special lady in my life. Looking back I am so grateful for her opening her toddler filled home to me. She gave me a great start and a safe place to start out on my own. She is still someone who would open her door if I needed her.

I opened the classified ads and saw an ad that read "Tuxedo company looking for a young, insightful person for their tuxedo sales department." I am sitting at my Aunt's table thinking, I am 18 years old and I could measure men all day! Ha ha! (The novelty of measuring men wore off over the years …)

The job was not all about measuring men. It was very hard work – scrubbing dirty rental shoes, picking through piles of BO-smelling tuxedos, digging in the pockets of dirty tuxedos (hoping you wouldn't find anything you didn't want to!!), ironing, altering, fitting and working in a very hot dry-cleaning plant. Plus the emotions of wedding couples who wanted their day to be perfect.

There were many 10%s but I loved the job and the people I worked with. I loved being a part of the wedding day of my customers. The 90%s outweighed the hard work and working conditions.

In the blink of an eye, I was 24 years old and I had invested the first six years of my adult life in what I thought would be a summer job. I was very blessed to be mentored by some incredible people who helped to shape me as an entrepreneur. It was the best university I could have ever attended.

Arriving at work one morning I saw a serious looking fellow in a blue suit in a heated discussion with the owners. The tuxedo company was going into receivership, on its way to bankruptcy. This ended up being a turning point in my life. I had always felt that if I got the chance there were some big changes I would make in this store. Four male co-workers and I sat in a coffee shop down the street and bounced some ideas around. We felt like we could do it and we took the chance. A month later we were the new owners.

My partners stayed to run the original store and I moved myself to a branch store 550 kilometers away. It was a new store for me. New city. New life. I needed it. A chance for a fresh start. I packed up my car with everything the bank didn't own and moved again. For old times' sake I popped in my "Whitesnake" cassette tape. "Here I go again on my own ... "

I learned very quickly in my new store that having a great attitude would help me run my own business. There were many 10%s as I built up the business, but the greatest gift I could give my clients and, most importantly, my staff, was someone positive to work with. I made lots of mistakes but I persevered and I had the honor of working with the most amazing people.

There was a bit of a buzz about this "young woman" who had come to town. Opening a tuxedo rental shop at 24 years of age was not what most young women did. I received a lot of media coverage and loved the opportunity to be interviewed and talk on camera. I was not shy and of course – I loved to talk!

One day, I was in my bank and the manager called me into his office. Ed was a kind man who always took the time to say hello and look you right in the eye. He became one of the many mentors who have helped to shape my career. He asked me a question that would change the course of my life. "I want you to speak at our next staff meeting. My staff are very interested in how happy you are all the time, genuinely happy - not delusionally happy. And you come in the bank and you are friendly to the staff and remember everyone's name. They want to hear how you stay so positive. Can you do that?"

I said, "Yes, I would love to." Then I remember leaving his office and feeling like I would throw up. Who wants to stand in front of people and talk? How did I stay positive? I remembered the book I had read "Attitude Is Your Most Priceless Possession" and my magnifying glass idea. I came up with the ratio of 90% and 10%.

Nineteen years ago, I stood in front of Ed's staff and shared my very first "Focus on the 90%" message. A man who worked at the bank called me to say his wife and her staff would love to hear me too. Well as they say ... "the rest is history." I began to speak occasionally when people would call me, but I was still running my tuxedo store full time.

A third business opportunity appeared. I was planning my own wedding to Darren, and in planning my own wedding I noticed that there were not enough Bridal Shows for the size of city we lived in. There seemed to be an opening for another Bridal Show – a wedding trade-show where brides could go and visit wedding-related booths and see a fashion show. Darren and I started our third business and we organized, produced and promoted our first ever "Most Incredible Bridal Show" in 1993.

Now I was juggling the demands of an ever-growing tuxedo store, a budding speaking career and an annual bridal show. I was receiving numerous awards for my entrepreneurial accomplishments, and beginning to study my path very carefully. What would have happened had I not taken the chances I had?

I was now 31 years old, running three successful businesses and I was pregnant. I had to make a choice. I knew that I wanted to be home for my children and I also knew I could not do everything.

I decided after 12½ years in the tuxedo industry, I was done. I needed to be done, I was getting burned out and it was starting to show to my staff. I knew that I needed to practice what I preached to my audience members. If your negative 10% list outweighs your positive 90% list, it is time to move on. And my time had come. I sold my shares to my partners, and that chapter of my life was closed.

I was ready to start my new life as a full time speaker, trade show promoter and mom. I set up my home office and adjusted to working alone after so many years in a busy store. I kept chanting 90% … 90% … 90%.

My speaking career boomed. In 22 months we had two angels, Jayda and John, to add to our family. Darren took "paternity leave" from his job and we traveled like crazy as I delivered my presentations in those months. After John's birth, Darren made a decision to quit his "good government job" to stay home full time and support my career and our traveling life. (I still think he quit so he could golf all summer!)

For years, I was a full time-speaker who traveled with my family. I don't know if that conjures up glamorous images for any of you but the reality is was not always easy. It had its 90%s, but it definitely had its 10%s too. I have traveled with sick children and sick me. I have traveled with a husband who did not feel well mentally every day. As I said, NO sick days for speakers.

I have packed and unpacked more times than I can count. I have "acrobatically" nursed my children in a moving vehicle (you moms will know what I am talking about!). Darren would wait outside of the banquet rooms with our babies and I would run out on the breaks and nurse my children during my presentations.

We have dealt with cancelled flights, lost luggage and have been rerouted to cities we'd never heard of. You name it and we have likely been there, intentionally or accidentally! I chose to travel with my family so I could be with them everyday. I also chose to do this because I share a very strong "family first" message in my presentations. If you are going to talk it, I figure you need to walk it too.

The 90%s of traveling as a family were many. We did not miss a day with our children and we have albums of pictures filled with the "adventures" we have been on. We have had many 90% adventures but of course we have had a few 10%s too … and they've been just as memorable!

Now that our children are in school full time, I commit to a very balanced travel schedule. I could work more than I do but there is a price to pay and I am not willing to pay that price.

I want to be the example to my children that work should make you happy. I can tell them or I can show them what it looks like to be in a job that you love.

*I have a saying in my office that reads "Peace. It does not mean to be in a place where there is no noise, trouble or hard work. It means to be in the midst of those things and still be calm in your heart."*

## Snow in May?

We were traveling in the prairies on May 12th. Jayda was three years old and John was one. We packed up the van as we had done so many times, portable DVD in place, snacks, crafts, toys, work materials, suit, cooler, strollers, suitcases, laptop … Whew … off we went!

Heading down the highway we started to get a few snowflakes. Snowflakes in May? If you are from the prairies you know how to drive in bad weather, so we forged on. The weather got worse and worse. May 12th!

The next morning I was speaking to 250 people 550 miles away! This was not good!

We pulled over in a small town to "let the storm pass" –only to discover that they have closed the highway in front of us. We get the last hotel room in town and it is definitely a 10%! The sign on the hotel room wall read: "Do not let your hunting dogs on the beds."

With two very busy toddlers, we need to burn off some of their energy so we headed out into the snow-covered town. There is nothing to do so we spend four hours at the local clothing store trying on everything they had in the store, and another two hours at the pharmacy looking at magazines and children's books.

We spent long meals in the restaurant and attempted to make our room a fun zone. We made forts with the blankets and chairs in the room. What else were you going to do with toddlers in a snowstorm?

I never did make it to the presentation the next day. When they opened the highway, we turned around and went home. When my friends and family asked, "How was your trip?" I said the same thing I always say, "It was awesome." I never complain about things I have no control over. What is the point of that? It is what it is.

When you look for the positive 90%s, they are there. When do I get to spend hours in a day just playing with my children in stores and blanket forts? When do I get to try on clothes for four hours? We ate the greatest home cooked-meals at the local restaurant – that I didn't have to cook! I discovered later that over 200 people were stranded and had to "camp out" in the church basement. Hey at least we had a bed! We were safe, fed and able to get back home. Why complain about it?

*Tommy Lasorda once said:*
*"Don't complain about your problems: 80% of people who hear them don't care. And the other 20% are glad you're having trouble."*

*Mr. Lasorda ... I agree!*

## Viva Las Vegas

I was invited to speak in Las Vegas by a Canadian company and I surprised Darren by inviting him along for the trip to celebrate our 10th Anniversary. Grandma and Grandpa came to stay with our angels for our first weekend away together since the children had been born. A second honeymoon!

For the first time in five years my husband and I sat on an airplane with no children! We arrived in our connecting city to discover that our flight was cancelled due to bad weather and the flights were backed up. I was to speak the next day in Las Vegas and this one I could not miss. The clerk at the check-in counter informed us that we should go over to ticketing and see if there was anything they could do for us. He yelled, "Good luck" as we bolted away.

I switched on my "positive attitude", and as we made our way to the exhausted ticket agent, I started with, "This must be a terrible day for you." With a deep sigh he said, "Yes." I joked with him as I explained our predicament. After pounding away on his keyboard for what seemed to be hours, he looked up and said, "I think I found you two stand-by seats on a connecting flight to another city. Oh, and one other thing, the flight has already began boarding and the gate is on the other side of the airport.

We were like participants on the television show "The Amazing Race" as we raced to the gate. We waited breathlessly until the last two standby seats were called, they were ours, we made it! Whew, only one more city to go and we would be in Las Vegas.

We arrived in our next city and again ran as fast as we could to the next gate. We just made it. This time we were on our way to Las Vegas.

We arrived in Las Vegas at 7:00 pm, six hours behind schedule. Guess what? ... no luggage. No ticket agent to be found ... no one in the "lost luggage" office. We were tired and hungry so we headed to our hotel. The concierge at the hotel advises, "You'd better go buy something. The luggage is not usually found." I take her advice since I am not a natural beauty and I need "stuff" to get ready for my presentation the next morning.

Things keep getting stranger and stranger. Our room number was 911. Our buffet ticket was 666. It was 8:50 pm when we arrived at the mall. I had always heard that Vegas never sleeps, but I never imagined the mall would close at 9:00 pm! We had 10 minutes to shop. Darren and I headed in opposite directions and threw together an outfit that was two sizes too big. No time to find all the beauty aids I needed!

Back at the hotel, I borrowed a curling iron from the woman working the front desk, I washed my face with the soap Darren showered with, and I rubbed hand cream on my face. So much for my "beauty routine."

I woke the next morning to discover the hotel's hot water heater had broken down. I showered in ice cold water and I delivered my presentation with a smile on my face and a safety pin digging me in the back. When I finished my engagement, Darren and I played the slot machines for hours – we figured our luck had to change! We didn't actually win any money but we had a great time.

Las Vegas has this great above-ground subway that you can ride on and see the entire strip. We decided to go for a ride to cap off our final night in Vegas.

At the first stop, Darren jumped off to grab some bottled water from a vending machine. He said, "I'll be quick." As he was watching the water drop down the machine, I was watching the subway doors close. I lunged towards the doors and just missed as they shut.

We were now looking at each other on opposite sides of the glass as the tram took off. My first instinct was to get off at the next stop and wait. Sounds logical doesn't it? Not to Darren. He decided it made more sense to wait where he was for me to come back.

So I am standing in a Las Vegas tram station at 11:00 pm on a Saturday night and I am in the company of some scary looking people. I am fearing for my life. As the train pulls up, I think well, Darren must be waiting at the first stop so I decide to get on the tram heading the other direction. As you might imagine, Darren has now decided to ride forward to find me!

To make a long story short, over an hour later, we finally connected at the same station. It felt like three hours. Let's just say I was not "focusing on the 90%" when we finally connected! And the honeymoon was definitely over!

We were flying home the next morning. We arrived in our connecting city to discover that the gate number on our ticket was wrong. We were again ... running ... through a huge international airport.

When people asked about our trip, my answer was – you guessed it! "It was great!"

We didn't become millionaires on the slot machines in Vegas, but we did make it safely to an engagement I needed to be at. I lived through the train station episode. We were particularly grateful when we contemplated what it would have been like to be running through airports with the children in tow! I learned a lot that trip – I always wear a suit on the plane and carry toiletries in my briefcase!

If I had come home from Las Vegas and complained to my friends who had been sitting in two feet of snow, they would not have cared. I was in Vegas, they were in snow!! Now, I have great loving friends - and I mean this as nicely as I can make it sound … they really don't care! We often complain about the 10%s of our jobs to people who have their own job 10%s too and they shouldn't have to care about ours.

*I love my job and I make a choice to be happy in a job that I choose to do. I choose this job, so why would I complain about something I am choosing to do? I could have many other jobs, I choose this one. I am always amazed when I meet people who seem to feel it's necessary to justify that they enjoy what they do.*

*I meet people who say things like "Don't think I'm nuts but I love my job" or "As crazy as it sounds, I*

*ACTUALLY really enjoy what I do." Why is it strange to enjoy your job? When I question these people as to why they would say " nuts or strange" to enjoy their job they tell me why. They say when they go out into the world and tell people they love what they do people look at them strangely.*

*I sit next to a stranger on an airplane many times in a year. They always ask me the same question, "What do you do?" I NEVER tell anyone I am a motivational speaker, no one wants to sit next to a motivational speaker on an airplane!*

*When they ask me what I do I always say the same thing, "I have a dream job. I love what I do." Invariably my passenger will say to me "Wow, you sure don't hear people say that very often."*

*Why not? Why do we live in a society where it is strange to enjoy what you do? Who started that?*

## Are you happy?

I was listening to a motivational CD and the message was from a speaker named Steve Rizzo. Steve said on his CD that if you are not happy … you are not successful. I had learned this at my dinner table.

So, I decided I would make a choice over the next few speaking engagements to pay attention to who was happy and who was not. Days later, I was on an airplane, sitting next to a very high profile businessman. He spent the entire flight telling me about what he "owned" in terms of material possessions.

Now since I had just listened to the CD, I couldn't resist the temptation to use this man as ... "research." So I told him the story about the CD and how I was in the process of gathering information from successful people about how "happy" they are. I asked him ... "Are you happy?"

A reflective look came over his face, he slowly turned and quietly said "No. I haven't been happy for years ... I have no marriage, I don't know my kids, I work way too much and I am on too many airplanes. I often brag about never taking holidays. As if that is some kind of badge of honor."

The rest of the flight his conversation flipped around. He shared stories of his family and how he needs to work less and connect more with them in order to be truly ... happy. Nothing he owned would be buried with him.

So Mr. Steve Rizzo, you are right. Success is a relative term. It means different things to different people. Success to me does not mean how much I make, where I live or what people say about me. Success to me means doing a job that I love and working "just enough" to have quality of life. It means that the personal relationships with people I love are strong and in front of everything else. I am speaker who never speaks about wealth. I don't care what you make or what you do for a living. I care about whether you are happy or not.

Are you successful? I guess you need to ask yourself ... are you happy?

*"Often people attempt to live their lives backwards: they try to have more things, or more money, in order to do more of what they want, so they will be happier. The way it actually works is the reverse. You must first be who you really are, then, do what you need to do, in order to have what you want."*
Margaret Young

## 3 years, 4 hours, 1 minute and 2 seconds left

I worked with a group of people who were suffering from low moral issues. The second person to arrive at the training session was a man who was clearly unhappy about having to be there.

The blank name tags were to be filled out with the attendees' first name. As I watched the group preparing I noticed that this particular man had written on his tag - 3 years, 4 hours, 1 minute and 2 seconds left.

Now I know that we count days to retirement for a variety of positive reasons but this gentleman's name tag went with his attitude. As I looked at that tag, I thought that it must be difficult to work with someone who is just biding their time.

When people tell me that it is our youth today who are struggling with being motivated on the job, I challenge that belief by asking, "Who is teaching them? Who do they get to learn from?"

Often today's young people are placed in organizations where they work beside (or worse, work for) people who are just counting the days that they will have left until retirement. Young people tend to start their jobs with enthusiasm and they get placed next to people who do not want to be there anymore. So it is not surprising what attitudes they are absorbing as they sit beside people like that all day. Knowledge is not power unless you are sharing it.

We have a choice to leave a legacy. What impression will you leave? Why don't you choose to go out with a bang? Will you be proud of your retirement dinner? Will you be proud of what your co-workers say about how they will miss you?

When I asked an audience the question, "Why did you choose this job?" A young woman stood up and said, "I chose this job because I wanted the opposite job my parents had – I never wanted to be as unhappy as they were everyday."

## Mentors

Mentors have shaped my life. The mentors in my childhood are too many to list. When I entered the workforce, I learned very early the importance of asking for help. The knowledge I gained from those who had "been there a while" I could not have learned in a textbook.

Everything I know today as an entrepreneur, a professional speaker and an author, I have learned from others.

If you are considered the "youth" of your group, reach out to the employees who have "been there a while" too. You can learn a lot from people. Some people in your workplace have a great deal of knowledge to share. All you need to do is ask.

*What about the others around us in our work and our personal lives? Can they affect our attitudes? Let's talk about them.*

*"Never lose sight of the fact that the most important yardstick of your success will be how you treat other people - your family, friends, and coworkers, and even strangers you meet along the way."*
Barbara Bush

## Others around you

*Do you think a negative person can bring down a group?*

*When I ask this question during a presentation, most of the hands will fly in the air. Most people can share their own story of "one or two" that they work with, grew up with or live next to ... who have affected them in a negative way.*

*I've been amazed by the number of people I have met who started their job with their magnifying glass on the 90%s. They couldn't wait to get that job. Then I would meet those same people a year later and they had changed. Now their magnifying glass had been moved to the negative 10%. What happened? Most say that one of the greatest influences that affects them and their ability to stay focused on the positive 90% is "the other people that I work with."*

*They start positive, but soon say it is the people, not the job, that affect how they feel about going to work each day. They say that one negative person can bring down an entire department or organization. People often tell me they leave other people, not the job itself.*

*I know in my own businesses that one or two negative employees can affect the morale of the entire group. So when clients would call me to speak and they would express concerns about morale, I wondered if they were dealing with the same issue. Could there be one or two in their group that were "affecting" the rest?*

*What about in our families, with friends and in our neighborhoods? How do we deal with those 10% people in our lives? I have met them, I know them, I have worked with them, they have worked for me, I have prayed for them and I have tried to love them.*

*So what do you do with negative, 10% people? I have spent years researching why people act the way they do and ways to live with them. I have learned this – as hard as I have tried to make people happy, they have to do that themselves.*

*I had a very close friend go through a very emotional weekend-long addiction recovery program with an addicted family member. One of the many things they learned that weekend was that they did not own the problem of the person with the addiction. This made a lot of sense to me. Not easy to do but it made sense. Only the person with the addiction owns that problem. I related that to the people who we can't seem to reach. People with a negative attitude own that attitude. It is not ours. We can't change people, only our reaction to them.*

*Only you can control you. That's it. We can't control others and their behaviors.*

*So what do you do to co-exist amongst the unhappy? The best way I have found is to see them through your 90% magnifying glass. Look past the behavior to the soul of the person.*

*My greatest learning lessons come to me from three different groups of people, my own children, passengers beside me on the airplane and audience members. One of the greatest learning gifts I received was from an audience member named Diane. Diane taught me to look past the behavior. She taught me that people who are unhappy on the outside are also unhappy on the inside.*

## "The B"

I arrived for a presentation with 100 attendees. We would spend the entire day together and we would share a morning session on focusing on the positive 90% of your job and those around you. In the afternoon we would "switch gears" and focus on themselves as individuals and their family life.

As I have said, I pride myself on being a customized speaker. I like to learn as much as I can about the company and the people that work their. What are their 90%s and 10%s? It is pretty hard to connect with people if you do not care who they are. I do not want to be a talking head telling everyone to be happy.

I interviewed a portion of the audience and I learned from many that they had an employee in their group they called "The B" (rhymes with "ditch" and is not positive). My first thought was, what a horrible name to give another person. What right to do we have to label someone with such a terrible name when we also have imperfections?

I heard stories about this woman coming in to work in the morning and going straight into her office without saying good morning to anyone. She stays in her office all day - hardly ever comes out for "coffee time" and never attends the special lunches the social committee arranges. As one woman explained in disgust, "And the worst part is, she never comes to the Christmas party."

It was clear there was a great deal of energy spent on this woman and her behavior. I learned that "The B's" name was in fact, Diane. I wondered if I would be able to pick Diane out. Sad, unhappy people are easy to find.

As the audience filled the room, everyone sat together in groups, with the exception of one woman, who chose to sit at the back corner of the room by herself. My guess was, I had found Diane.

I shared my morning message focused on the work portion of our life. I then shared my message about others and how we all work with "one or two" difficult 10% people.

I wrapped up the morning session and it was now time for lunch. We all piled into the cafeteria and again … 99 people sat among their colleagues and friends and Diane sat alone. It was as if there was an imaginary "cope" shield around her that was keeping people away from her – and my guess was, it kept her from having to deal with others too. Now as I watched Diane sitting alone God called on me to go and sit with her. I didn't really want to sit with her, I would rather sit with the "happy people" but I figured I had nothing to lose. I do not have any agenda with how she has treated me and don't have to work with her for the next 20 years. Besides … she is research for me!

I walked with my tray full of food to her table. As she looked down eating her meal I asked the top of her head,

"May I eat with you?" With one swift move, she kicked out the chair across from her and said, "It's a free country, do what you want." I was a little afraid but I had come this far!

It was obvious this woman was hurting. So searching for something to say I said, *"My name is Darci."* She looked up from her meal, looked me right in the face and said point blank, *"Stop."* She went on to say, *"Something I did not like about your presentation this morning was that you refer to us unhappy people as 10% people and it is obvious who the 10% is here, isn't it?"*

I was taken a back and my pride was hurt, but I have a thick hide and I am always interested in improving myself. I want my message to have an impact so I asked her, *"What should I have said?"* I moved to the chair next to her so I could let her speak quietly.

She started out by saying, *"Well I know what they call me here … and it hurts. There is nothing worse than being gossiped about when they do not know my story.*

*"You know Darci, I have worked here for three years and no one has ever given me the time of day. I am not saying that I am an approachable person but you would think that in three years someone would at least reach out a bit. Maybe I deserve to be treated this way but I honestly do not know how else to act right now. I act this way because I am barely coping with my life. My personal life is hell.*

*"I wake up in the morning next to a man who has been passed out drunk for years. My husband lost his job due to his alcoholism and I had to get this job. If that isn't stressful enough, I walk down the hall to my 17-year-old daughter's bedroom and stand outside that door before I open it. You see, my daughter has gotten in with the wrong crowd. Sometimes I open that door and my daughter is not in there. I spend my morning making calls trying to track my girl down. Some days I feel like I am barely coping with my day and it is only 7:30 a.m.!*

*"I put my suit on, I put my lipstick on, I look at myself in the mirror and I say to myself, Diane, you can do this one more day. I know I should "lay that sucker out" and get help, honestly Darci I do not know where I would even start. My dinner table is the dinner table I grew up at. I swore I was going to do things differently than my parents. How can my daughter learn anything about taking care of herself when she does not have an example to live by?*

*"I arrive at work and I rush into my office and … hide. Work is the only place I do something … right. The only place in my life I haven't screwed something up. I don't come out for coffee because I don't have the energy to listen to everyone complain about their job. This is a great place to work. They should feel lucky we have these jobs and quit complaining.*

*"I don't come to the stupid lunches they put together because I am so sick of my co-workers complaining about their petty lives and their petty marital problems when my life is so full of*

*problems. I feel like saying to them, 'Come home with me for a week, I'll show you marital problems.'*

*"She looked at me and said, "And Darci, how am I supposed to take my drunk husband to a Christmas party?"*

I am a crier. I am a hugger too. I love to hug people … especially those who are not huggers - it is like hugging a piece of plywood! I reached over and hugged Diane. I figured, maybe it had been a long time since she had one.

I went back in front of this group for my afternoon session and here is what I said:

*"You know the 10%ers in our lives? What if we viewed them through our 90% magnifying glass rather than through our 10% glass? What if when we saw another person we chose to see the positives in them first?*

*"No one in this room is perfect. We all have our faults, we all have our stresses and we all have … a story. What if we cut each other a bit more slack and tried to view each other in a more positive light? What if we recognize the fact that we may not know what is going on in some people's lives that may be causing them to act the way they do? What if we take the time to care and have compassion and empathy for another human being?"*

*"What if we remembered that work is the happiest place some people go in their lives. It is true people who are unhappy on*

*the outside are unhappy inside too. Would it change a 'culture'? Would it create more 'team atmosphere'?"*

The manager emailed me to say they heard my message loud and clear and they would work on their kindness to Diane. I prayed they did. I also prayed that Diane would get the help that she, her husband and their daughter needed.

**Think about the 10% people in your life. Could it be possible to look past their behavior to the soul and see what might be going on in their life?**

*"Never look down on anybody unless you're helping him up."*
Jesse Jackson

**When my entrepreneurial friends say, "My staff are not happy." I always ask the same thing, "Are you?" Are we showing our staff what it means to come to work full, happy, rested, and caring for others? Or are we showing them something the opposite of what we are asking them to be.**

*The greatest example we can set is to be the exact example of what we want them to be.*

## Maybe it is you who is changing?

I told the story about Diane to a Christian group and after my presentation I received an email from a woman who told me that they too had a "Diane" within their group. She shared in her email that after my presentation the group started a prayer circle for their Sheila.

Every time they caught themselves gossiping or being rude to her – a very un-Christian thing to do – they would say a prayer for Sheila instead. The woman who emailed me said, "It is so amazing Darci after a month of being kinder and praying for her we thought to ourselves ... wow ... Sheila is changing."

I emailed her back and said, "No she isn't – you are."

When we change how we "view" others – we choose to see them in a more positive way. A 90% way. Isn't it our greatest calling as Christian people to love others as we are loved?

When someone calls me and says, "I hate working with him, he is such a jerk.", I listen three times. I hear their side and try to empathize. On the fourth time, I lay that sucker out and say, "I am sure he is not an easy guy to work with but I guarantee you something, there is more to this guy than his behaviour. He must have something else going on in his life that is causing him to act so awful at work."

Is it ok for him to act like a jerk? Of course not.. But we also have a choice. We can see just the negative side of his behaviour or we can see him through a 90% lens and question, "I wonder what else is causing this behaviour?"

I have been blessed with many gifts and pride myself on being very intuitive. When I meet people, I often think to myself, I wonder when they are going to work on their 10%s? We are all great actresses and actors in the world but if we do not deal with our personal problems, it comes through in our personalities. It affects how we treat others and ourselves.

Remember, you can't change others, you can only change you.

My beautiful sister Amy once sent me a magnet that reads:
*"Before you criticize another person you should walk a mile in their shoes, that way when you criticize them, you are a mile away ... and you have their shoes!"*
Ha ha.

# Changing me ...

*When I started to realize that I could not change the 10% people in my life, I set on a path to change my view of them. To view them through my 90% magnifying glass. I started to read and research what I could do to change my reaction.*

*I learned that our judgments of others cause most of the problem when we are trying to connect and be compassionate. Most of these judgments we learned at our dinner tables. I have had to reframe how I view some people. I know compassion cannot grow in a judgmental heart.*

*My dad said when I was a child I was always asking "why?" Every answer he would give me, I would respond with "why?" I am still asking "why?" Why do people act the way they do?*

*Did you ever notice that those who judge others and gossip about them are actually the ones who need the most work? A great way to avoid your own problems is to focus on everyone else's. Then you do not have to look in the mirror at what might be part of the problem.*

*Two books that really set me on a path of learning are Debbie Ford's book "Dark Side of the Light Chasers" and Byron Katie's "Loving What Is." They both made me realize that it is how I react to people that is really the problem and perhaps part of the problem is actually me. I challenge you to ask yourself "Why does it bother me that this person is negative?"*

*Others reflect back to us parts of ourselves that we do not like or better yet parts of us that still need some personal development work. I am a firm believer that if everyone did their "work" and looked after their self-esteem issues and their personal challenges; we would have far greater morale in our workplaces and in our personal lives.*

*Not everyone is going to like you. I have found that most of the reason this bothers me is my own self-esteem issues. I wanted everyone to like me but that is not realistic.*

*I am working very hard at raising a daughter who grows up knowing that women love and support each other. Women grow up with beliefs they learned at their dinner tables. Beliefs like, "good girls make everyone happy" or "women give a 110%." Maybe they were wrong, maybe we can't make everyone happy.*

*Unhappy people are sent to me for a reason, a test to see where I am in my personal growth and a test of my compassion for others. Can I love the unlovable?*

*Think about most of the movies we watch, there is a mean character. Even in Disney cartoons, there is someone sent to test the goodness of the others. There is always a bully. Good prevails over evil.*

*Why in real life do we let them win so often?*

"How people treat you is their karma, how you react, is yours."
Wayne Dyer

# Compassion

I am always working on having more compassion for others. I also love to observe human behavior and "10%" unhappy people. It is so true; there is always more below the surface.

In the airport, I was "observing" a man who looked angry and depleted. We were in line to check our suitcases and he was already agitated. He wasn't very friendly to the smiling WestJet agent.

In the short security line, he complained about the length. And then the unthinkable happened. Security found a full-sized shaving cream in his carry on. I took a step away from my "behaviorally challenged" flying friend as he reluctantly handed over his $3.00 shaving cream. The guy behind me in line muttered to me, "Does he have to be so rude?"

I observed him in the waiting area sitting alone, staring out the window like he had lost something. I reflected that it looked as if he was looking for a piece of his soul.

He walked up the aisle of the plane and I realized that he was going to be my neighbor. He forcefully shoved his suitcase in the overhead and slumped with a heavy sigh into the seat next to me. I smiled to myself and thought, "this is definitely a chance for some one-on-one research – another lesson is seated beside me."

I respectfully gave him the cool down time he needed. (Remember, not everyone is excited to sit next to a "Motivational Speaker"). After a few minutes, I started. I always look for a way to connect so I said, "Those overheads are never big enough are they?" As he turned to agree, I could see the pain in his eyes.

We spent a few minutes exchanging "surface" conversation – the weather, the economy, our jobs and then I asked him about his family. He told me about his crumbling marriage and his broken relationship with his son. He teared up as he told me his boy was in with the wrong crowd and doing some of the wrong things. On top of all that, his job had changed and now he had to travel every week in a time when he really needed to be home.

We spent the rest of the flight talking about his boy and I reminded him that in all that he is doing, his boy needs to know he loves him. I gave him a much-needed hug (I hug everybody) as he departed and prayed for him and his family.

If you look deep in the eyes of the unhappiest people you meet, you will see their pain. The pain people show on the outside pales in comparison to what they feel inside.

Now the rude guy in the airport was a human with challenges and feelings.

I know it is not easy to deal with, work with or live with unhappy people but the ability to see them with compassion, with a 90% view, has transformed how I connect with others. This is something I am always working on, how well I connect with the 90% people AND the 10% ones. Maybe the 10%s need that connection even more than anyone else?

Should unhappy people do what they need to do to be happy and treat others better? Yes, definitely. But some people are truly coping and doing what they need to do to get by. Often people did not learn at their dinner tables how to cope and take care of themselves first.

When I had a difficult employee, I would hear their concerns three times then I would ask a question that really worked for me.

"I hear what you are saying and I have heard your concerns with an open heart. The question I want to ask back to you is … "WHAT WOULD MAKE <u>YOU</u> HAPPY?"

This question often caused my staff to take a step back and look inside themselves for the answer. Often it was not work, it was something else in their life they were not willing to face.

Most of my employee's concerns over the years had nothing to do with work. They were personal problems that were coming to work with them.

*Try it. Next time that "one at work" or that "in-law" is being rude, look deep for the pain – past the 10% behavior – to the 90%, the soul of the person. You will see it.*

*"If you want others to be happy, practice compassion. If you want to be happy, practice compassion."*
Dalai Lama

## Teachable Moment

I am constantly challenged to look past the behavior of the 10% people and to the soul. Jayda and John and I visited a retail store and the staff were very rude to them. I ran a retail store for many years and I have been in business a long time, so I completely understand how children can be in retail stores. I remember all too fondly how the ring bearers would come into my tuxedo rental store and knock over mannequins and re-merchandise my entire store. Mind you a few groomsmen did that too! (Ha, ha.)

Now don't get me wrong, I know that our children are full of energy. I often say if you think your children are busy, just spend an afternoon at my house with our joy-filled children and you might reconsider!

In this particular 10% retail experience, our children were great. Truly, I am not delusional, they were great. They have been on dozens of airplanes and eaten in dozens and dozens of restaurants and they know how to act in a store. I am not saying there have not been 10% days, but this was not one of them.

There were three retail employees who repeatedly told my children not to touch anything, not to lean on anything etc. And they WEREN'T! They were simply waiting for me to finish and pay.

So as nicely as I could muster in my "motivational speaker" way, I patiently explained that I did not feel my children were touching too much and they were simply leaning to wait for me. The employee announced that they have had "problems with children in the store." We paid and left.

Now the discussion in the car with Jayda and John was based around how can we be friendly, caring and patient to the unkind. How can I defend my children without being rude to an obviously depleted woman?

Jayda and John felt very rattled from the experience and both exclaimed that they would NEVER go to that store again. I shared with them what we had talked about many times before; the hardest thing to do is to love the unlovable. I believe that negative people are "sent" to test our kindness and patience. Will they win?

I reminded them that we did not know what happened with other children in that store and we did not know what was going on in these women's personal lives.

We turned this 10% experience around in the car by sharing a few teachable moments.

#1. Jayda and John saw their mom stick up for them. Something children need more of.

#2. We learned how not to treat children when they have their own businesses some day.

#3. We prayed for those women.

As much as I wanted to be very impatient with the staff, I remembered I can TELL my children what it looks like to be patient or I can SHOW them. Being positive is great, I work very hard at it but the greatest challenge I have is being a 90% person in 10% situation.


*"It is understanding that gives us an ability to have peace. When we understand the other fellow's viewpoint, and he understands ours, then we can sit down and work out our differences."*
Harry S. Truman


## True, Necessary and Kind

I am a Christian and interested in other religions and beliefs. I read an article in Whole Living magazine asking readers to share their best ideas and a reader wrote in sharing an excerpt from the book "Ethical Wisdom: What Makes Us Good" by Mark Matousek.

He shares a belief that you should ask yourself three questions before you speak: "Is it true? Is it necessary? And is it kind?"

I am the type of person who needs to cool down before I talk. If I don't, invariably I say things I regret. So before I talk to someone about how I am feeling I take a step back and ask myself those three questions.

Is it true? Sometimes when I am "feeling" something, it's my feeling and not theirs. And honestly, sometimes, the reason I am upset at someone is because they said something that was true. And upon reflection I learn that is what bothered me after all...they were right!! And my ego wanted to be right instead.

Is it necessary? Once I cool down I often feel it's not even worth bringing up. Is it worth talking about something that happened a week ago? Is it worth dragging it back up? I know people who gunny sack their anger. I believe that will make you sick. We have to learn to let it go and forgive. I am not perfect. Neither is anyone else. I love the saying "resentment is like taking poison and waiting for the other person to die."

Is it kind? I would never ever treat a client disrespectfully, so why would I treat the people I love, work with and are friends with any differently? Before I open my mouth, I say the words in my head, "Is this a 90% kind thing you are going to say?" If not. I try not to.

"If you have nothing nice to say, don't say anything at all."

Sometimes after asking these questions, the answer is "yes." It is true, necessary and kind to share my feelings or express my views. Not everyone is going to agree with everything I say or do but as long as I am true to me, it's okay.

I have typed these three lines up and printed out two copies. I put a copy on my desk and one in my wallet to remind me of these profound words before I speak. Am I spreading forgiveness, patience and love by how kind I am being to others?

*"Beginning today, treat everyone you meet as if they were going to be dead by midnight. Extend to them all the care, kindness and understanding you can muster, and do it with no thought of any reward. Your life will never be the same again."*
Og Mandino.

## Two Wolves

I have been blessed to speak at First Nations events where Elders are invited to start the day. One of the First Nations Elders I met read this to open our day.

*One evening an old Cherokee told his grandson about a debate that goes on inside people. He said: my son the battle is between two wolves inside us all.*

*One is evil: it is anger, envy, jealousy, sorry, regret, greed, arrogance, self-pity, guilt, resentment, inferiority, lies, false pride, superiority and ego.*

*The other is good: it is joy, peace, love, hope, serenity, humility, kindness, benevolence, empathy, generosity, truth, compassion and faith.*

*The grandson thought about it for a minute and then asked his grandfather which wolf wins?*

*The old Cherokee simply replied; the one that you feed.*

**Viewing people through the 90% magnifying glass has transformed the way I view people. My stepmom, Sandy, laid a great foundation for me by showing me that everyone has a story. She is a kind woman who always sees the good in others. She taught me many things and she taught me that people are doing what they need to do to get by. She is one of those people who get along with everyone and accepts people just they way they are. I strive to be like her.**

**People deal with depression, health issues, aging parents, divorce, teenagers, debt, addictions … the list goes on.**

**I have learned in my own healing journey that everyone is on the mission in life they are supposed to**

*be on. I have a hard time accepting that sometimes. When someone hurts another person, especially a child, I have a hard time practicing compassion. But even then, I have tried (sometimes it is really hard) to understand that people act the way they know how. They act out how they were treated.*

*The nicest people I have met treat the smallest of the world the kindest. It is always a reflection of the character of a person by how they treat a child.*

*People lead big lives. Everyone has a story. I honestly wonder how some people get out of bed. I do not know how some people who have been through so much, are able to function in the world. How some have scrapped off their childhoods, endured their negative marriages and suffered in so many ways and they still cope, is beyond me.*

*I don't care if we are 20, 40 or 60 years old, we all come from something that has shaped us, 90% and 10% events. Some of us not only have a "story" but we have a TV mini series - full of romance, horror and comedy!*

*Some of the happiest people I meet are ones that have been through a lot of personal crisis in their lives. Not to say there aren't happy people who haven't had crisis but the happiest I have met have dealt with a lot. People who have been to hell and back always rise a little higher. It is as if going through a personal crisis makes you stop and realize how precious life is. I am a living proof of that!*

*When people complain a lot to me I often think they probably have not had a lot of personal crisis. When we have a lot of crisis we build a resistance to the little stresses in life. When you have had big things to complain about, you complain less about the small things.*

*Similar to our health, why does it take a crisis for us to realize that life is short? Why don't we stop and realize that life is great now?*

## Happy enough to slap

Some of you reading this are very positive people. Some of you are the ones who pump everyone else up. Kudos to you. Being positive is not easy. I know this firsthand. Working with or being with negative people when you are trying to stay positive is not easy either. Stay strong. You don't own it, you can only control you. Keep your self-esteem high and your heart filled with compassion so that you enter interactions with others a full positive person.

When people joke about the woman in the room who is "so happy we could slap her." I always say to the group,

"Who would you rather work with, her, or someone who drags themselves to work?"

I am known as an optimist, which annoys a certain percentage of people. (Maybe 10%?) I know the ripple effect that my attitude has and I make a choice to be positive. What is wrong with Pollyanna?

Being positive is not always easy, when you tell a co-worker they are "too happy", you actually put their light out.

***What are you known as at work? Are you a 90%er or a 10%er? Trust me, you get known as one or the other.***

*"If you want to be happy, be."*
Leo Tolstoy

## We have to get along!

When staff groups say to me "we are like a family" I always jokingly say "OH NO!" I personally have grown up in many different families and they all hold some degree of dysfunction! Seriously, if your group is "like a family", I say, lucky you!

At an association conference, a group of employees from one office were having such a great time. The entire morning that I shared my message they were having the most fun.

At the break I asked them, "How do you all get along so well?" A few around the table shared with excitement how they had all worked together for years and they loved working together. I shared with them that it is remarkable because sometimes people who work together all day sometimes lose the enthusiasm for each other.

One woman from the table stood up and said proudly , "We live and work in a small community. We have no choice, we HAVE to get along!"

As I walked away I thought, what a great attitude! Imagine if we implemented that within all groups? Families do it all the time. What if we decided we just HAVE to get along!

But what if we can't? What if we have done all the work we need to do as individuals and we have tried all we can to get along with a negative co-worker and they still affect us. I would question if it were time to move on and find another group to work with. No one else's unhappiness should affect yours.

People say that if you quit a job to get away from a negative person, that negative person wins. You know what I say... who cares! If you have tried to be loving and compassionate and someone is affecting your peace of mind you should be proud to walk away. Remember you can't change them. You can only change you.

## Creating a happy workplace

I have made an observation about families that I relate to work groups. I have noticed that when children grow up with really loving parents, the children are usually pretty close. BUT if children grew up with parents who did not do a good job of being loving and supportive, the children seem **extra** close. It is almost as if they subconsciously said, "If we are not going to get the love we need from Mom and Dad, let's be each other's support."

I think we need to band together in work groups where we feel the "leader" is not giving us the love we need and be each other's support. Don't wait for "Mom and Dad" to make us happy. Be that for each other.

*"Without great employees you can never have great customer service."*
Richard F. Gerson

# Leading your staff with a 90% view

Viewing people through my 90% magnifying glass has transformed how I manage and lead my staff. Viewing our staff members through our positive 90% magnifying glass is a powerful way to build people up. I was not always good at this. The more I took care of my own self-esteem and cared for me, the more I could care for them.

Self-esteem is a fragile thing and we as leaders are responsible, in part, for the self-esteem of our employees. We need to make choices to see the 90% positives in our employees first. How we treat our employees is how we send them home. If we deplete them in the day, we send them home depleted to their own families.

I remember that my staff member is someone's child. This person is someone's spouse or partner. They could be someone's mom or dad. How I treat them is how they go home to their special families. My incredible assistant Sandra is someone's daughter, her husband's wife and her daughter's mom. If I were a fly on the wall during their dinner table discussion, I would want to be proud of what she says about how I treat her.

We need to work on our own self-esteem issues so that we can feel happy and full so we can fill others! I have had the honor of meeting many leaders across the country and the leaders who are stand out as 90%ers are the ones who are looking after themselves, mentally, physically and spiritually.

Like I said earlier, we grow up with belief systems around how to treat others and ourselves. We learn that good girls make everyone happy and women give a 110%. Men grow up believing that they do not talk about their feelings and big boys do not take pills. These shape and form how we feel about ourselves and then how we treat others.

We have intolerance of others based on our own beliefs. If we see someone who is not performing to our 110% standard, we judge them as inadequate. I would challenge what we feel about others. Is it a shortcoming in ourselves?

We as leaders have a responsibility to be "full" as I mentioned in my first chapter. Mentally , physically and spiritually. It will be very difficult to lead a productive team when we are depleted. Actually I think it is almost impossible. How can we build culture with people who are depleted?

We grow up with beliefs around taking care of ourselves too. We learn that those who ask for help are weak. They were wrong. You need to be full to fill.

In the book, *"What Happy People Know"* Dan Baker Ph.D writes: "There are some people who derive pleasure from ordering others around, but they're just insecure people who have no real personal power: power over their own lives. People who run their own lives do not need to run others."

Once we accept and love ourselves, we can accept and love others. Most of us have worked for someone who depleted us. I bet if you knew their personal lives you would learn why they came to work and tried to control. I bet if you followed them home, they would treat their own children the way they treated you.

When I take responsibility for calling that employee into my closed office and asking them if they are in fact ... okay? Something amazing would happen. When they know you care enough about them to ask, and you have built trust, they would share. Like I said before, I have never had a concern with an employee at work that did not have problems within their personal life. Late to work all the time can reflect a bigger problem at home.

I started to see my employees with more compassion and empathy. I have learned that work is the happiest place in some employee's lives. I now take my role in their happiness very seriously.

I love the John Maxwell quote that says, "See your people as they could be, not as they are."

## How are you?

I remind my leaders in my leadership presentations to NEVER ask how anyone is, unless you truly have the time to listen to their response. There is nothing more disconnecting than being lead by someone who you know does not genuinely care about you.

A man emailed me and shared with me that he was that manager. He was the guy who went up and down the assembly line of his company and often asked his employees, "How are you?" And it hit him. He never listened to their responses. So now he not only tries to be the guy who makes an appearance, he is now the guy who listens, too.

He shared with me, "Now, I only go out on the line when I know I have genuine time to listen. I don't try to talk to everyone. I talk to a few and hear how they truly are."

One of my best friends Cari manages a hotel with many staff members. When a staff member is hired, they fill out a questionnaire that helps her to learn about them. It includes all of their favorite things, how they like to be acknowledged, etc. She will reference that sheet to do special things for her staff. She has taken the time to care. No surprise, she runs a very successful business with happy staff members.

How do we treat our staff members? Do we call meetings to only discuss the 10%s? What if we had 90% meetings and discussed what was going well? Do we thank our employees in person and by email? What if we started every day with a 90% meeting? What if we ended the day the same way?

Our employees should go home at the end of the day, full for their families. They should feel like they were appreciated and cared for. Wouldn't happy employees improve the customer service delivery in your business?

*"The day soldiers stop bringing you their problems is the day you stop leading them."*
General Colin Powell

## No Morale Issues

I am not saying that morale issues do not exist but here is what I have found. When morale issues exist there are a percentage of the employees who are having personal problems. Big personal problems. And what happens when we do not deal with our personal problems, is that they come to work with us. Then we are trying to create a culture of motivation and happiness with people who are depleted in their lives.

My compassion grows week after week for how much people deal with. I know life is stressful but we need to be accountable for dealing with our personal lives so we can be happier. I sit next to people on airplanes all the time who share their personal challenges with me. I listen empathetically then often ask them, "What are YOU doing to cope with your life?" So often they can not answer that. When we are living with stress we often forget we have choices on how we cope with it.

When we do not deal with our problems/challenges which we all have, someone else will pay the price for that. They pay by how we treat them. We can pretend we are okay but your coworkers and staff know you are not. Do something to move forward. It is impossible to come to work depleted by our lives and expect to add fullness to the work place.

I know it is hard to look at our 10%s and change. I know first hand the hardest person to change is the one in the mirror.

And I know for sure, those organizations that I speak to that have very few issues with low morale, also have a group of employees (starting with their leader) who is committed to their own happiness.

I believe that if we all dealt with our personal problems on our own we would be happier and then we would go to work happier and everyone would not have to suffer for our lives. Morale issues would become less of an issue. And wouldn't that be a wonderful place to work?

*"Morale is self-esteem in action."*
Avery Weisman

***So what do YOU need to do to cope so that you can add to the positive morale where you work?***

## Listening

Listening is a wonderful gift. And it is hard to do. Especially for those of us who love to talk. It is one of the greatest ways to create a connection with those we work with and those we love.

People say to me all the time, "I am a terrible listener. I never remember anyone's name." My challenge would be; did you truly listen when you asked their name?

It astounds me how many times I sit at a luncheon with a staff group with their manager present and discover how little the manager knows about his/her employees. I will go around the table and ask people their name and some questions about themselves. Often the leader at the table will say, "Wow, I didn't know that!" in response to something his staff says. I sit there wondering, What do you ask these people and are you really listening when they talk?

## Traffic

There was a time where even in traffic I would get upset if someone cut me off. I now wonder, what is going on in their lives? When I was pregnant I used to drive and think, "What if my water breaks and that guy will not let me in to get to the hospital?" So now I view all drivers that way. What if the woman driving is pregnant and needs to get to the hospital? What if the man driving is going to meet his pregnant wife at the hospital? I let everyone in on that premise. I realize that pregnancy isn't likely the cause of all the rude driving but the principle is the same. I try to cut people a little slack.

When I am in the car while Darren is driving, he lets everyone in with a wave – and he mutters to me with heavy sarcasm, "Ya ya I know, her water is breaking."

Have you never been late? Have you never been rushed in the car?

I once heard a comedian say, "When you are feeling frustrated behind an elderly person for driving slow, just imagine if they drove fast."

It changes how we see others if we see them in a positive 90% way.

When a cashier/waitress/serving person is rude I cut them some slack too. How do I know how they are being treated at work or at home? I stopped at a Prairie restaurant and the sign behind the counter read: **Be kind to our waitresses they are harder to find than our customers**. What a nice message to send to their staff.

When a young person does not seem to know their job, I offer patience. I view them as someone else's child. How would I want someone to treat my own child in that situation?

## An email from Bill

*"The day after my wife lost her battle to cancer I was driving somewhere (probably shouldn't have been behind the wheel!) and I went straight through an intersection on a turning arrow. The guy coming towards me with the right-of-way went ballistic (fist shaking, swearing, etc.) and all I could think about was what he would say about his own behavior if I told*

*him why I had screwed up. I remind myself of that day when someone does me wrong."*

## There is always one

Early in my career a client invited me to speak to his employees. I arrived for the engagement and the manager met me outside the training room door and wanted to warn me that he had a couple of employees who were causing some low morale issues. He explained to me how these two; Bonnie and Tom might not treat me properly as a speaker and I should be prepared. I reassured him that I was ready and he kind of pushed me into the room wishing me a "good luck."

As I walked past the back table to make my way to the front, a woman announced as I walked by, so loudly that the entire room could hear, "What does she weigh, like 80 pounds?!" She caught me off guard and I looked her way.

Each of my audience members receives a mini-magnifying glass to remind them of my message and on the back of that magnifying glass is my picture. I looked down at the table in front of the outspoken woman and saw that she had doodled on that picture – on my face! She blacked out my front teeth, drew a long goatee on my chin and big devil horns coming out of my forehead! I noticed her name tag ... it was Bonnie. The man sitting next to her was – no surprise, Tom.

While I was up front delivering my presentation, Bonnie and Tom ... visited. They laughed and carried on like I was not even in the room. Bonnie blew big bubbles with her gum. You could feel the tension in the room and I could tell the affect they had on the others.

What amazed me was that obviously these two had already decided before I even arrived what they thought of me and the training evening. Long before I arrived they had their magnifying glasses on the 10%. The second thing that amazed me was how this pair was acting in front of their boss! I wondered if they learned at their dinner table as children that where you work will not make you happy and that bosses did not deserve respect.

When we regrouped after the break I asked the question, "Do you believe a negative person can bring down a group?" Guess who put her hand up first? Bonnie. I am standing up front thinking, she is part of the problem and she doesn't even know she is a problem. She can't even see her own negative attitude.

No matter how hard you try to love, pray for and care about ... there will still be one or two people who choose to keep their shield up. Those who seem to "rock everyone's world", the ones who really do not think they are the ones with the problem.

I have also met clients like this. Ones you can't seem to make happy no matter what you do for them. Let's talk about them.

*"Customers don't expect you to be perfect. They do expect you to fix things when they go wrong."*
Donald Porter, V.P. British Airways

# Your clients

*I don't think it is realistic to keep 100% of clients happy. In fact, I think it is impossible. I also think it is an unrealistic expectation we put on ourselves, and our staff – that we can make everyone happy. I think 90% is good enough.*

*But don't we tend to focus on the 10% who will never be happy no matter what we do? We spend 90% of our time on those 10% of our clients, some of whom were probably never going to be happy in the first place.*

*I have seen many companies who have policies in place to cater to the 10% not the 90%. I have to take my shoes off at the airport because of one guy! I can't take water on the airplane because of one person. Don't get me wrong, I am happy for the safety at the airport! But it shows how we cater to the 10%.*

*I speak at dozens of conferences in a year. I sit in on the presentations before it is my turn to speak. I have watched as countless displays of customer service survey results on slide shows. I have never seen a company that boosts 100% client satisfaction. Why do we think we can achieve it?*

*Just like the unhappy people around us in our lives, I think unhappy clients are sent to test us. If all of our clients where happy, we would become complacent. If it was all 90%, we would never appreciate it. 10% clients shake us up enough to ask if we should be improving. That way we do not become complacent.*

*And then there are clients that are just plain rude. No matter how hard you try, they are "entitled to give their opinion."*

## People pleasers

I think it is hardest on the nicest people. When they try really hard and a customer still is not happy, it has the greatest impact on them. Often because they are so committed to pleasing others and maybe they grew up at a dinner table where they were taught to make everyone happy.

Again, it is impossible to keep everyone happy and we will become exhausted in the process. I often remind people that if we have the courage to do whatever we do for a living, we have to be willing to catch the 10%s that come with it.

I always say I have to have a thick enough "hide" to catch what people think of me. If I can't handle that, I need to stop speaking. There will always be someone who doesn't like what I say. If I show up with respect for them, enthusiasm for what I do and a message I am proud of, isn't that good enough?

## Your comments are important to us

In my busy speaking months, I stay in a lot of hotels. You know that little card in the room that says, "Your comments are important to us?" The one where the hotel asks you to please take the time to fill it out and let them know how they did?

Well, I have decided to take the time to do that as many times as I can. I have decided that I will take the time to fill that card out, do the on-line survey or email them back, because I ask audience members to fill out an evaluation form telling me what they thought of my presentation. The least I can do is return the favour.

Since I am a positive person, I like to take the time to write the positives of my stay. Not only do I write a positive or two or even three, I take the time to find out the name of any staff member who impressed me with their service. I tell them that I speak on attitude and customer service for a living and I think they did an exceptional job and I tell them why we enjoyed our stay. You can find a positive if you look for it.

I have now filled out dozens of those comment cards and email forms and I take the time to do this even though I don't really have time. In the early days of traveling with my family I would be sitting at the desk in the hotel room filling out the card while Darren was trying to get out the door with two, yes count them, two luggage carts filled to the top. Jayda and John are anxious to escape and run down the halls. Needless to say, Darren wasn't always supportive of me doing this in the midst of the chaos of getting out the door to catch our plane. Now I travel 90% of the time alone, I still carry on the tradition.

Why do I bother? Because I think it would be really nice for a hotel and its employees to hear something positive because people tend to complain on comment cards. I also know that some managers have not been to the Focus on the 90% seminar and do not share positives with their staff. It could be what an employee needed to hear. Who knows maybe they live in a house where they never hear any positive comments. Why else? I am interested to see how many will respond to my positive comments.

Of the dozens of hotels we have stayed in year after year guess how many of them have responded to my glowing comments? If you were an optimist you would say 90% responded, right? Some of you would say 10%. In fact, very few have replied. Sometimes I get the generic email one back, but a genuine thank you back, very few.

When I tell this story in my workshops, many of my audience members tell me stories of times of when they have stayed a hotel and they had not been happy with the service and complained. They tell me stories of getting a free room upgrade or flowers or chocolates in the room. Some have told me about surprise packages full of toys for their kids to play with! Huh?? So is the message that if I had complained instead, I would have received free things for my family?

Many people say to me, "I bet you if you had written a complaint on those cards you would have heard back!" Sadly, they are probably right. But isn't that what we tend to do? Focus on the 10% of our customers who are not happy, rather than focusing on the 90% who are? The squeaky wheel gets the oil.

I know we can learn a lot from our unhappy customers. We can learn great ways to improve our business but if we spend all our time on them, we forget about the ones that are already happy. If we do not make them feel appreciated, they will find someone else who does.

I have asked people who manage hotels, "Why am I not being responded to?" I have been told that when the pile of comment cards arrive on their desk on Monday mornings they pick through the pile and find the unhappy 10% comment cards first. By the time they finish putting out fires with the 10%s, they have no time left to deal with – and thank – the happy 90% comment cards like mine.

Sound familiar in your business? We spend so much time trying to make happy the unhappy customers that we often forget about the happy ones. No, the customer isn't always right – 10% of the time they are just cranky.

*Take a good look at where you spend your energy. Is it on the 90% or the 10% of your customers? What can you do to make your 90% customer feel appreciated and wanting to come back? I would highly recommend a simple thank you not combined with a holiday greeting. Not a computer generated thank you letter, something hand written and special. If you have a large client base, just thank a few.*

"Silent gratitude isn't much use to anyone."
G.B. Stern

## Say Thank You

Maybe your gramma told you (as mine did!) "If you don't have anything nice to say, don't say anything at all!"

I've always thought that was pretty good advice. But what if we do have something nice to say? Then I think we should say it! I think that is truly "focusing on the 90%."

In my opinion, one of the nicest things we can say is "thank you." How often do we say thank you to others? In our business?

Just think about your own business for a moment. When I share my customer service presentation, I often ask my audience members if they thank their clients or customers. They always respond with "Of course!"

But when we really think about it … do we?

I can't tell you how many times, as a hotel guest, I've thanked the front desk staff as I check out. They cheerfully respond, "You're welcome!"

I've finally realized that this process is backwards. What am I thanking them for? For allowing me to stay in a room that costs more than my first 1968 Volkswagen Beetle and provided only slightly more amenities?

I've eaten far too many meals in restaurants where the serving staff respond to my thanks with an automatic

"Come again", and draw a happy face on the back of my bill.

When a client comes into our business, I think one of the first things we should say is "thank you." Seriously. When I walk up to the reservation desk at a hotel, what if the person waiting for me smiled and said, "Before I check you in, Mrs. Lang, I want to say thank you for choosing our hotel!" Or when I sit down in a restaurant, the server said, "Hi, thanks for coming in tonight."

It will take your business to another level if your first words to your client – whether they're looking for a loan, wanting to buy a house, or seeking a speaker for their next convention – are, "Before we begin, I want to say thank you." Each client is our pay-cheque. We need to do a better job of letting them know how much we appreciate them.

So let's make it a point to "focus on the 90%" and thank our clients. Saying "thank you" is truly saying something nice!

*"The smallest act of kindness is worth more than the grandest intention."*
Oscar Wilde

# The Accountability Agreement

I spent the first few years of my life working as a manager not really sure how to manage and not thanking enough. Most people are not trained for this position. I spent a lot of time focusing on the negative 10% of my staff. I would come in the morning and find what was not done, point out what they did not do well. I was what Kenneth Blanchard in his book "One Minute Manager" calls a Seagull Manager. Someone who flies in, squawks at everyone and leaves. Then I learned the power of Focusing on their 90%s and it transformed how I lead. If I look back most of why I acted the way I did was because I was insecure about my role, I was young and over compensating for my lack of experience.

If my staff were doing the best they could, what more could I ask of them? They were only 90%. No one was perfect, but again, neither was I.

I learned as the years went on that there were just a certain percentage of clients who were never going to be happy. We could have shoved $1000 bills in the pockets of their rental tuxedos and some of them would still have found something wrong.

I decided that if we really provide our customers with the best possible service we can, we should not feel stress. I really mean that. This led to the development of the "accountability agreement."

My half of the accountability agreement would be that I would promise each staff member that I would be the best leader I could be for them. I would arrive with a smile, I would try my very best to focus on their positive 90%s and I would be the example of what I was asking them to be.

Much like with our children, when leaders tell me their staff are not happy, I ask them "Are you happy?" We can tell our staff what we expect of them, or we can show them what it looks like to be a great service provider, etc. Whatever we are asking them to be, I ask, "Are we the true example?"

Their half of the agreement would be that they would be accountable to me and the business. I would ask them to promise me that they would give the best possible service they could to our clients with a positive attitude each day. Okay, almost each day. Our clients were expecting the best possible service for their wedding day and how they looked for that special day was very important to them.

I always worked Mondays because that was the day the tuxedos were returned and the day you heard any complaints. Inevitably someone would return unhappy. It was a high variable business and many things could go wrong with a rented garment. Some days I could feel the spit hit my face as a customer yelled at me about his broken tuxedo pants and how they practically fell down while he was walking down the aisle. (Maybe you are a member of the "sworn at by your customer club" in your business too?) I would listen, empathize and do whatever was needed to fix the unfixable. If at any point of his yelling at me he said anything negative about a member of my staff I would politely say to him, "I know we made a mistake but I trust my staff and I know they did the best they could."

When the customer left, happy again – most of the time, I would ask my employee, "Did you give this customer the best possible service you could? Did you triple check the pant clips and the measurements?" She would always honestly answer yes. I would tell her then to go home that night and feel no stress. If you give the best you possibly can what more can I ask of you? But the flipside was this … if any employee was honest with me that no, they did not do the best they could, those were the times they felt stress. When their part of the accountability agreement was not in place.

*How accountable are you? What level of service do you provide?*

**Think about the percentage of your customers who are happy with the service you provide. If you don't know, it is a great idea to ask. If the satisfaction rate is around 90%, you need to stop being so hard on yourself. Ask yourself, am I doing the best I can? If the answer is yes, lay your head down at night and sleep**

*peacefully. **Work through the belief system that you have to please everyone.***


## People People

The greatest service providers I have met have two things in common, they are happy with themselves and they love people. They have done enough of their personal development work that they can connect with others with compassion and care.

When people say to me "I am not a people person", I say then please do not serve the public for a living. I recommend they go and work in a field with animals and never come out and serve real humans again. Haven't we all been served by someone who was not a people person? Why would we take a job that does not match our personality?


## Walter

I had so many people who believed in me at the beginning of my work career. One of the many things I did was travel with my tuxedos to small town men's wear stores and "pedal my wears." I would meet the owners of the stores that rented tuxedos from our head office location.

Putting faces to the voices on the phone. I learned so much about customer service on the road.

I loved that responsibility! I was met with an interesting variety of responses. I was very young and as one store owner put, "very female" in a very male world.

I learned so much from those store owners. I learned very early that if I made my age an issue, they would too. I was proud of what I did and I knew my stuff. That is all they needed to know.

One of my favorite owners was Walter. He was a kind, grey-haired man who always greeted me with such enthusiasm. He amazed me. When I would wait for him in his store, I would watch him work his magic. He was calm and intentional and his smile warmed your soul. He knew everyone's name that came in, what they bought last time and a bit of their personal life. You could tell that he was well loved by his clients.

I grew up believing in the importance of asking people who know more than you, how they do what they do. As I said before, mentors shaped my life as a young entrepreneur and they do today as speaker. So one day I asked Walter, "How do you remember everyone's name and how do you know so much about your customers?" I wanted to be like him and I wanted to learn more about how he conducted his business.

Walter said, "I will teach you." With pen and paper in hand ready to write down his words of wisdom, I waited and he said, "Do you want to know the secret?" I nodded enthusiastically. He simply responded, "I care." I was 18 and not sure that it was a very good response but 25 years later I have come to see the wisdom in Walter's words and I still think about that special man's advice.

Those words stay in my heart to this day. I think about that when I work with my clients. Do I care enough to listen? Do I care enough to learn about the man and woman, not just the person looking for a speaker? Every time I am introduced to someone, sit next to them on an airplane or listen to my children after school, I ask myself, "Am I caring?"

We are so inclined to jump in, finish someone's sentence, want to be right; processing our own response or wait to tell them how terrible our life is in comparison to theirs. What if we didn't? What if we just listened? What if we just cared?

*"Caring is a powerful business advantage."*
Scott Johnson

## Itchy pants

I started in the tuxedo business delivering tuxedos and ended up owning my own tuxedo rental store. I rented tuxedos to thousands of men. Renting tuxedos was not an easy job but it was very rewarding. I loved my job.

I cared very much for my customers. I met men at pivotal moments in their lives, ring bearers in the family wedding, as graduates and as grooms.

Five-year-old ring bearers would run around and destroy my store and were so proud to be in their first tuxedo.

Eighteen-year-old graduates were preparing to head into their adult life. It was such a shock to see them out of their baggy jeans and in their handsome tuxedo.

I met grooms from all walks of life. Some were excited, some nervous and some were unsure if they were making the right decision! I can't tell you how many talks I had with grooms and their feelings. It was very important work to me and I took it very seriously. How you look is part of your self-esteem, especially on your wedding day. I was in charge of that.

If the mom of any of those three groups of men would come with their "boy" to my store, she would always cry when her boy came out of the fitting room. It didn't matter if they were five, eighteen or twenty-five, the moms would cry.

Though society might not have thought owning a tuxedo business was important work, we thought it was and we cared very much about what we did.

Few men I know forget their graduation or wedding tuxedo rental experience (good or bad!).

In our busy peak season, we would average a few dozen customers a day. Most would be happy. In a week there would always be one or two who weren't. It was inevitable. No matter how hard we tried, there was always that unhappy 10%.

You know what I wanted to say to the bride who was about to marry Mr.10%er don't you? RUN!!!!! I tell all my brothers and sisters how your date treats the waitress on your date, that is the future of how you will be treated.

And who would my staff and I talk about on our very rare coffee break? (If you have worked retail you know, breaks can be rare!) Of course, the 10%! Not the happy customers. We had dozens of thank you cards and wedding pictures posted on the wall. We would get flowers, pies and chocolates as gifts. But we did not tend to think about that. Our focus always leaned towards the ones that we could not make happy.

I would get home at the end of a long retail day and when Darren would ask me how my day was, I would talk about the one or two, not the pie and chocolate!

I used to lie in bed at night and think about ways to get back at those 10% customers. What if I made the crotch of his pants itchy for his wedding? ... (Just kidding!)

Since I am always interested in people's moods and why they act the way they do, I decided to use my customers as research and here is what I gathered. The first thing that I gathered was – something that did not surprise me when dealing with this cranky groom – four out of five of his groomsmen were rude to me too. People surround themselves with what they know. Look around at your friends; they reflect exactly where you are in your personal development journey. If you hang out with depleted unhappy people, you don't have to improve either. After all, misery loves company.

What did surprise me though was that about 90% of the time when his dad would come in for his tuxedo fitting, his dad would be rude to me too. The apple does not fall far from the tree. People act the way they are taught to act at the dinner table. People learn at their dinner table that retail employees do not deserve respect.

I started to realize how unrealistic it was to try and keep everyone happy. Some people are never going to be. I could probably have called the limousine company, the hotel the wedding was booked at and the florist and ask them if they had dealt with this particular 10% groom I was having trouble with. I'll bet you, they would have had a problem with him too.

So we changed what we talked about on our coffee breaks. I changed what I shared at my dinner table with Darren.

Now don't get me wrong. We made mistakes. My gosh, we rented tuxedos!! That was just the makings for mistakes! I am talking about the people we were trying to do our best with ... and it just wasn't good enough. That taught me that some people are just never going to be happy.

It also taught me that my staff were not perfect, and neither was I. It was how I handled their mistakes that kept their self-esteem high. People need to hear that they are good. They do not need to only hear the mistakes they make. As I said before, work is the happiest place in some of our employee's lives. For some it is the only place they hear something positive.

When we would have a cranky tuxedo customer we just high five each other when he left the store saying "Thank God we aren't marrying him!"

I have met a lot of great men in my life. I was raised by one; I am married to one; I have measured many and have spoken to thousands. As I said earlier, the quality that I admire the most about a man is his ability to treat the smallest of the world the kindest. Men who treat children, animals and those who "serve" them with kindness are the greatest men I know.

I was always amazed when a customer would be rude to my dad in his Volkswagen business. They would treat him as if he worked for them. Even back then I would think "You don't even know how to change your own oil and you're being rude to my dad?"

I often remind people that if you grew up with a belief system that you are "entitled to give your opinion" remember... that opinion ripples to someone else. If you have demanded to see a manager because the waitress did not serve you properly, remind yourself, you have no idea what is going on in that waitresses life. And before you complain, ask yourself, "Have I ever made a mistake at work? Have I had an off day?"

*"Be kind, for everyone you meet is facing a hard battle."*
Plato, Greek Philosopher, Mathematician, and Philosophical Writer

**When you didn't like my tuxedos and we had made a mistake it was tough on me because I really cared about my clients. I understood that 10% was part of the business but when I became a speaker and an audience member didn't like me that was different. It felt more personal.**

*A few years into my career, I realized how important it was to gather feedback from both my client and my audience members.*

*I have learned so much about how to improve my message ... and my delivery from my audience members. I am committed to continual growth and learning.*

*When I needed help to improve my tuxedo business, I sought mentors. In our bridal show, we are always asking what can we do to improve the show. As a speaker, I have hired coaches, attended boot camps and I am committed to constant improvement on the platform. There will always be something to learn and grow from.*

*You have to really ask yourself sometimes, is there some truth in constructive and helpful criticism? It is impossible to be perfect but what can I constantly be learning?*

*I always think it is wonderful that magazines post their unhappy readers comments in and amongst the glowing ones. That is reality, not everyone will be happy.*

## It's all about the hair

I was invited to speak at a Women's Conference. I was the first speaker in a full day line-up of speakers. It was my job to "pump them up" and start the conference on a positive note. I arrived around 6:30 a.m. at the ballroom, which was incredible. The sun was rising and pouring warm orange light into this ceiling-to-floor-windowed room. I had about an hour to myself in the room to prepare and I prayed that God would use me as he needed to that day. The sun was now streaming into this beautiful ballroom and dancing off the crystal chandelier. It was one of the most magical rooms I have been in and no one had even arrived yet.

At 8:00 a.m. the first of the 250 women started to arrive and the energy started to build. Pack 250 women in a room and you are bound to feel some great energy! This group had paid their own money to come together as women for a much-needed women's day.

I deliver many presentations in a year to a variety of different audiences and since I am not perfect I sometimes deliver presentations that do not go that well. I always get paid and the clients are happy but I know in my heart it could have been better.

Not that day. Everything worked that day. The audience was warm and inviting. During the "sharing" portion of my presentation I had women telling stories of overcoming cancer, losing children and many stories of how women had decided to be happy in their lives by focusing on their positive 90%s. It is always amazing to me that the people who have been through the most in their lives seem to rise above it all and live life to the fullest. Like I said, those who have been to hell and back, rise higher.

It was an emotional, meaningful morning. There were women hugging and crying. You could feel the estrogen pumping through that crowd!

The three hours together ended with a standing ovation and a long line of hugs from audience members. I knew that I had delivered a purposeful presentation that day. I was selling and signing books and CDs in a flurry of activity. I could hardly get out of the room! I felt like Tony Robbins!

Afterwards I had women emailing me, telling me what they did differently after they had heard my message. Managers who went back to their workplace and passed out my mini-magnifying glasses to their staff and started a 90% culture in their work places. Women who shared how they went home and slid that magnifying glass across the dinner table to their spouse and said, "I want us to find the positives in each other again." Mothers who realized they had not told their children enough how much they love them. Everyone truly did have a story. Powerful stuff. I even had a husband email and say, "I don't know what you said to my wife but she is sure nice to me today!"

I assumed that since it was such a meaningful presentation, the response that I received from the women in the audience would be positive. And it was. I received 249 heartfelt evaluation forms from women who shared their life stories with me. Positive, glowing comments about what they were going to do differently in their lives after hearing my 90% message.

And then I was down to the last evaluation form. I assumed it would be as positive as the others were, but what I read was, "You sucked and your hair is too big."

I sat back in my chair, totally stunned. I felt sick to my stomach. Sucked? Who would write something like that? I wanted to email her and say, " You think this is big – you should have seen it in the '80s!"

What short-haired brunette would say that to me? No big-haired woman would say this to another big hair! How depleted is this woman? Where is her self-esteem at? What table did she grow up at and learn how to treat other women? Remember you can only see others as you see yourself.

At that moment Darren walked in the office and could tell I was upset. I handed him the evaluation to read.

After reading it, he fell on the ground laughing. He laughed on the floor for five minutes. When he regained his composure, he asked me what the other 249 said. I told him how great they were.

Then he said, "You are upset about this one email? Hon, three things: number one, one out of 250 is not 10%; number two, you probably look like her ex-husband's new wife and number three, no matter what happens on any stage on any week, we still love you the same when you get home."

And he walked out of the office.

Now my Darren is only right 10% of the time (ha ha) but I sat there smiling, thinking, "He's right."

As I said before, I love my job but it is just that – a job. It does not fully define me, it is simply one of the roles that I play. Being a wife and mother far exceeds anything I do as a speaker.

What I focus on in the day determines what I have left for the people I love. If I spend my evenings playing the movie of my day over in my head, focused on the 10%s I will be drained.

I choose to look at the 10%s that happen in a day and put it in perspective. I can't keep everyone happy and I am not going to try and be perfect. There will always be 10%, but there is always 90%. Where is your focus?

*"The Bigger the Hair, the Closer to God"*
Sue Buchanan's book title.

As I said at the beginning of this chapter, if I show up with respect for my audience and my client, enthusiasm for what I do and a message I am proud of, isn't that good enough? I am very proud of what I do. I spend a lot of time getting better at my "job."

When I get home from my presentation confetti does not fall from my ceiling and a red carpet does not roll down my driveway. No matter how much "success" I have had on the road, all they care about is whether I come home happy. My family loves and supports me but when I get home the question usually is,"What's for dinner?"

I have had the honor of speaking to many audiences and the esteemed honor of speaking to other speakers like myself. I have asked them, "What if we couldn't speak anymore? What if we didn't get standing ovations and sign our autograph, would we still be ok?"

My work can be good for the ego but I have to remember, this is my job; it is not my life. Being a speaker is simply what I do. It is a part of the woman that I am.

So when we drive home from what we do all day, we need to sit in that car and do two things. Number one, put the 10% into perspective. Ask yourself, "Did I do the best I could?" If not vow to change that next time and let it go. Then spend the rest of your drive thinking about what did go well. Focus on your 90%s that day. By the time you get home to your "doorknob" make sure you are giving your family the best of you. Turn your phone off, leave your laptop at the office and be fully present for your "life."

No client has the right to ruin your evening. Don't let them. Learn from it, grow, dust yourself off and enter your house full, not depleted.

# Epilogue

So my reader friend, we've had a great journey together. And some of you reading might be thinking, I know this – I know I should be more positive. My challenge is, will you do something with this idea? Will you take the time to imagine that magnifying glass in front of you and make a choice to see what is 90% positive in all areas of your life?

People say to me, "I have read 100 motivational books and seen a lot of speakers." I always ask them, "Did it work? Are you happy?"

When I run into people in public who say, "I saw you speak last month and it was just great", I always say a heartfelt "Thank you." Then I say, "I am so grateful for your comments and that you enjoyed the presentation but were you able to take the message back with you in your life and **do something with it?**"

It is great to know the message, but will we do something different as a result? I hope you will. I hope this book was like battery cables to jolt you into a new direction.

**Take care of you first.** Love you. Love your 90%s. Forgive yourself. I don't know what percentage of your life you have lived yet but do what you need to do to feel better and live life to the fullest. You never know which day may be your last. Do not waste another one. What are you waiting for?

**Love your family.** Give them your greatest 90%s. My grandpa used to say, "There will not be a U-haul behind your hearse." You can't take what you own with you. Only the love of the people in your families. Do not live one more day with guilt. Give the best of you to the people who matter the most, not your leftovers.

**Go back to your work** and make a choice to focus more on the 90% positive. Life is too short to drag yourself to work everyday. Leave a legacy. Be remembered as someone who came to work and made the best of it. Be grateful to be employed.

**Look at the people around you** with a new perspective. People do have the ability to affect us but let's rise above that and choose to be positive. View people through your 90% magnifying glass. Everyone is dealing with their own

10%s. Choose to be a positive person with others. Let's live our lives so that our funeral is full of people who's lives we have touched.

God Bless.

Focus on the 90%

## Meet Darci Lang

In her over nineteen-year career as a motivator and trainer, Darci has been invited to speak to numerous conferences, staff functions, development days and government departments across the continent.

A positive attitude is the foundation of Darci's success. She has owned and operated three separate companies, and managed a diverse and varied range of employees. As the present owner of X-L Enterprises and previous owner of an award-winning tuxedo store, Darci understands that working effectively within an area or unit requires you to work on yourself first.

Her dedication and entrepreneurial skill have paid off. She has also won the Saskatchewan Woman Entrepreneur of the Year Award and an Achieving Business Excellence (ABEX) Award. She was a finalist for the Canadian Woman of the Year Award and a three-time nominee for the nationally recognized Entrepreneur and Young Entrepreneur of the Year Awards.

Darci makes her home in Regina, with husband and business partner Darren and their two children.

She is truly someone who walks the talk.

Focus on the 90%

Focus on the 90%

Focus on the 90%

**DARCI LANG**
**Focus on the 90%**

Order Form

| Item | Per Unit Price | Number required | Total |
|---|---|---|---|
| Darci Lang "Focus on the 90%: One simple tool to change the way you view your life." | $20 | | |
| Darci Lang "Focus on the 90%" Live CD | $20 | | |
| CD & Book Set | $30 | | |
| Sub Total | | | |
| GST (5% of Sub Total) | | | |
| PST (5% of Sub Total, Saskatchewan residents only) | | | |
| Shipping and Handling ($3 for each Book or CD; $7 for each Book/CD Set) | | | |
| Order Total | | | |

**Order and Payment Options**

Order Option

Mail to:
XL Enterprises
P.O. Box 32077
Regina, SK
S4N 6E0
or
Fax to:
(306) 569-1356

Payment Option

❏ Cheque or money order (payable to XL Enterprises)

❏ Visa
Cardholder name: _____
Card #: _____
Expiry Date: _____

❏ MasterCard
Cardholder name: _____
Card #: _____
Expiry Date: _____

Delivery/Contact Information

Name: _____ Phone (___) _____

Address: _____

City: _____ Prov./State: _____ Postal/Zip: _____

Phone: _____ E-mail: _____

Ph: (306) 569-1354 Fax: (306) 569-1356 E-mail: info@darcilang.com
www.darcilang.com

Focus on the 90%